*Grey Feathers*

*Grey Feathers: Led by Love of Country — 2nd Edition.*


Published in the United States of America.

ISBN Paperback: 978-1-958030-14-1
ISBN eBook: 978-1-958030-15-8



ReadersMagnet, LLC
10620 Treena Street, Suite 230 | San Diego, California, 92131 USA
1.619.354.2643 | www.readersmagnet.com



*Cover design by Ericka Obando*
*Interior design by Dorothy Lee*

# GREY FEATHERS

## Led By Love Of Country

*2nd Edition*

**DANIEL DeWALD**

*Figure 1: $4^{TH}$ Division Unit Insignia*

*Figure 2: Vietnam Wall Washington DC*

# ABOUT THE AUTHOR

**DANIEL M. DEWALD** was born in Fort Wayne Indiana and served in the US Army 4th Infantry Division in the Republic of South Vietnam from August 1969 to August 1970. He had the rank of 1st Lieutenant and served as a combat platoon leader. As a result of the war, he received commendation medals for his activities. He received the Bronze Star Medal for Value (BSMV) for going above the call of duty when he saved the company commander and four others under hostile fire conditions. He then led a controlled withdrawal from the conflict. He also received the Silver Oak Leaf Cluster for conduct beyond the call of duty that occurred under hostile fire during a joint operation with the Army Republic of Viet Nam (ARVN). He received an Air Medal for participating in 25 combat assaults, a Combat Infantryman's Badge that was earned when he engaged hostile enemy fire, the National Defense Medal, the Vietnam Campaign Medal, the Vietnam Service Medal, two overseas bars, and served in a unit (4th Division that received a unit citation for its service.

Mr. DeWald received his BS degree in Business from Indiana University Kelly School of Business, Bloomington Indiana having graduated from ROTC. He also received an MBA from Xavier University, Cincinnat Ohio.

- Professionally Daniel's accomplishments include:
- Chapter President in the Association of Operations Management (APICS)
- Certified Production Inventory Manager, (CPIM) through the Association of Operations Management (APICS)
- Certified Maintenance Reliability Professional (CMRP) through the Society of Maintenance Reliability Professionals (SMRP)
- Certified Plant Maintenance Manager (CPMM) through the Association of Facility Engineering (AFE)
- Certified Purchasing Manager (CPM) through the Institute for Supply Management (ISM).

Prior to entering the consulting field, Daniel has worked with and for many blue-chip companies including Bosch, Marathon Electric, Chase Brass, Tower Automotive, and Navistar in Material Management. During his career Daniel has gained depth of experience in the Automotive and Trucking industry, Foundry, Electric Motor and Generator Manufacturing, Metal Stamping, Aerospace, and Injection Molding industries.

Since 2003 Daniel is a management consultant specializing in materials and distribution management. He develops courses on Maintenance, Repair, and Operation Supplies (MRO) and the storeroom, and conducts webinars and seminars on many topics, including ABC management, Cycle counting, and critical success factors for a storeroom.

He has published three books. The books are: Maintenance Storeroom and MRO Made Simple, Reliability-Web, 2012; co-authored Kitting in Maintenance Made Simple with Jeff Shiver, Reliability-Web, 2014; and Grey Feathers: Love of Country, SBPRA, 2013.

# DEDICATIONS:

To my mother Mary and my Dad Paul who encouraged me to research and provide a story about experiences in the Vietnam War. To my wife Sandy who put up with long nights of writing, talking about the war, and bringing up some sad as well as happy experiences. Mary, Paul, and Sandy Passed away. May they Rest in Peace.

# PROLOGUE

This book is based on after action reports, 4th division newspaper reports, personal observations, interviews, books, and discussions on the war effort in the years 1967, 1968, 1969, and 1970. The men who operated in the 3rd Battalion, 12th Infantry and 4th Infantry Division served proudly. There were many hardships in those years, and horrific combat conditions. The men responded well and with gallantry. They served with honor and integrity. The purpose of this book is to describe combat situations and the response of the 3rd Battalion, 12th Infantry soldiers to the adversities.

North and South Vietnam were separated by a demarcation line at about the 17-degree latitude above the equator. It was not a straight line but followed the roadbed of highway 102 The North was bordered by both China and Laos, and the South by Laos and Cambodia. The infiltration routes were through Laos and Cambodia, as well as by the sea. In addition, there were other insurgents in the country of South Vietnam, namely Viet Cong and Montagnards.

The Viet Cong (VC) were guerilla fighters that were against the South Vietnamese government. They used tactics of hit and run, and intimidation. The VC used AK-47 rifles, rifle propelled grenades (RPG), and mortars (60mm and 82mm) to hit quickly and escape. They would disguise themselves as farm workers, U.S. base workers, retail clerks, and truckers during the day, but a VC commando at night. It was almost impossible to distinguish a Viet Cong from villagers, unless someone from the village recognized them and let the U.S. soldiers know.

The Montagnards (a specific tribe in the Central Highland region) separated themselves from the population by living in separate villages. They lived in primitive thatched roofed huts on stilts. The men were the providers and excellent hunters. The women took care of their homes, cooking and cleaning. They would prepare the meals after the hunt was completed. In other words, the tribe lived a simple life, away from modern conveniences and communication. They pretended to be neutral in the war. Each village usually had a chief, to whom everyone recognized. He was usually the eldest and believed to be the wisest. Like all tribes, they would hunt, farm and fish for food. Yet, they would also be mischievous and set up booby traps to stop troop movements. The most common booby traps were the spear trap, pungi stick, or animal traps with pungi sticks placed at the bottom of a four-foot-deep hole. The VC learned from them and duplicated these traps, plus others.

No one knew for sure what side the Montagnards supported. They appeared peaceful, but actions proved contrary to that. Their weapons were mostly cross bows and spears. Many of the tribes were unfriendly to anyone who would visit them. They did not follow the laws of the South Vietnamese government, as they had their own set of rules to follow. The VC often recruited their tribe members to become insurgents by dragging the young men from their village and then forcing them to go against the West and the South Vietnamese government.

South Vietnam was in the crossroads of a political upheaval. The North Vietnamese were anxious to gain control of the South. The South had wealth, minerals, rubber plantations, oil, and a population who was not afraid to work hard in their fields. The South Vietnamese government would collect taxes on the villagers that most felt to be excessive. The taxes that were collected were used for other things rather than infrastructure, roads, agricultural subsidies, job training programs, and education. The other things were the improvement of the wealth of the government and the wealth of those government officials. Educators were not given the funds needed to improve the schools. The government was more a dictatorship, without labeling itself that. The West however believed in this government, and wanted to stop the insurgency through military means, as well as through civic action programs to "win the hearts and minds of the people." The goal was to preserve the South Vietnamese government and get a stronger government in place that was not corrupt and on the side of the people. It was clear that it was a war of Communism vs. Democracy and that it was important for the US and its Allies to preserve and protect the government as a matter of security and principal.

The state department theorized that a domino effect would occur if the South Vietnamese government fell to the North. Other countries would fall as well and then all of Southeast Asia could become Communistic. President Dwight Eisenhower began assisting the South Vietnamese Army by sending "advisors" from the military in 1955 to train troops and prepare them for the war effort. The advisors were overwhelmed at the task they were given, and in 1962 under President John F. Kennedy, troops were sent in addition to the advisors to help fight the insurgents.

This assistance with troops, advisors, and support lasted until the withdrawal in 1975, under President Gerald Ford.

The United States involvement was to strengthen the Vietnamese Army, Navy, Air Force, and Marines, and to help the South Vietnamese government be more successful in governing and becoming a democracy. Another reason was to prevent the spread of communism from China. The Chinese were involved also in the training and supplying of weapons to the North Vietnamese. Chinese and some say Russian advisors were often placed in the North Vietnamese (NVA) units.

There were many heated battles in the conflict. The military performed as well as it could be expected. The services (Army, Navy, Air Force, and Marines) were well-coordinated, and supported one another. Vietnam was divided into five areas of operations, commonly referred to as Corp areas. The 3$^{rd}$ Battalion, 12$^{th}$ Infantry was in the II Corp area of operations. The jungles were triple canopy, and difficult to maneuver. The Delta areas were wide open, and troops walked many hours through rice paddies and streams. Soldiers were given a week's reprieve from the conflict by the offering of Rest and Recreation trips to Australia, Thailand, Japan, Hawaii, and others. The more seriously wounded were evacuated to a Navy medical ship or to Japan, then on to the US for further recovery. The tour was for one year of service in country.

I have a great deal of respect for those that served, those that lost their lives, and those that were wounded and living with the wounds for the rest of their lives. The Vietnam Wall in Washington, DC is a reminder of the more than 58,000 lives that were lost in the war. Some of those who served were captured and spent time as a Prisoner of War. This openly displays the sacrifice and the hardships endured. Each name on the wall has a story, but also those that survived the war also have a memory of the events encountered. All are heroes in my view, and all of them should be recognized.

# TABLE OF CONTENTS

# CHAPTER ONE—INTRODUCTION

## *Gulf of Tonkin Resolution*

The Vietnam War had not been approved by Congress as a declaration of war. It was referred to as a "police action." The reason for this action was to stop North Vietnam (considered a Communist government) from overthrowing the South Vietnam government. It was believed other countries in Southeast Asia would follow and become Communist governments (referred to as the "domino effect"). A "police action," not a War action, would assist the Vietnamese in defending themselves and to provide security for the country. A declaration of War must come from Congress, and so the term War was not politically used in reference to sending troops to South Viet Nam. "Police action" was a term used for an undeclared war. In 1964 the Gulf of Tonkin resolution was signed. This doctrine gave President Johnson the authority to conduct combat without a declaration of war. A summary of the resolution is as follows from Wikipedia:

*"The Gulf of Tonkin Resolution' (officially, the Southeast Asia Resolution, Public Law 88-408) was a joint resolution that the United States Congress passed on August 7, 1964, in response to a sea battle between the North Vietnamese Navy›s Torpedo Squadron 135 (Moise 1996, p. 78) and the destroyer USS Maddox on August 2 and an alleged second naval engagement between North Vietnamese boats and the U.S. destroyers USS Maddox and USS Turner Joy on August 4 in the Tonkin Gulf; both naval actions are known collectively as the Gulf of Tonkin Incident....... It is of historical significance*

*....... giving U.S. President Lyndon B. Johnson authorization, without a formal declaration of war by Congress, for the use of "conventional' military force in Southeast Asia, and...... authorized the President to do whatever necessary in order to assist "any member or protocol state of the Southeast Asia Collective Defense Treaty". This included involving armed forces."*

The unanimous affirmative vote in the House of Representatives was 416–0. The result from this resolution was that it gave the authority for the Lyndon B. Johnson administration to begin its rapid escalation of U.S. military involvement in South Vietnam and to conduct open warfare between North Vietnam and the United States. The number of troops involved in the conflict escalated to over 500,000 troops in country in 1969. President Johnson did not run for a second term in 1968.

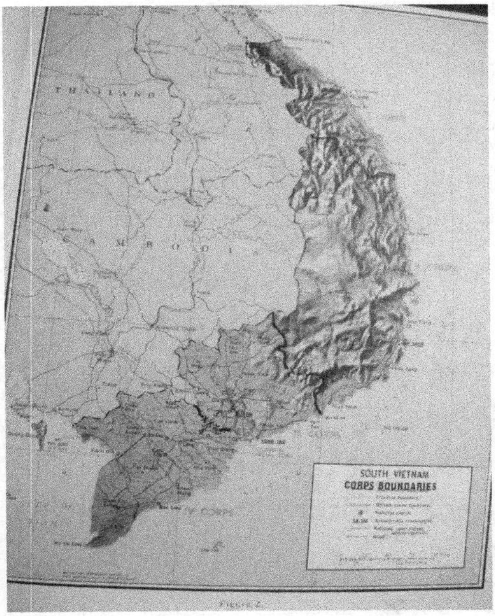


Figure 3: Map of South Vietnam showing Corp Boundaries

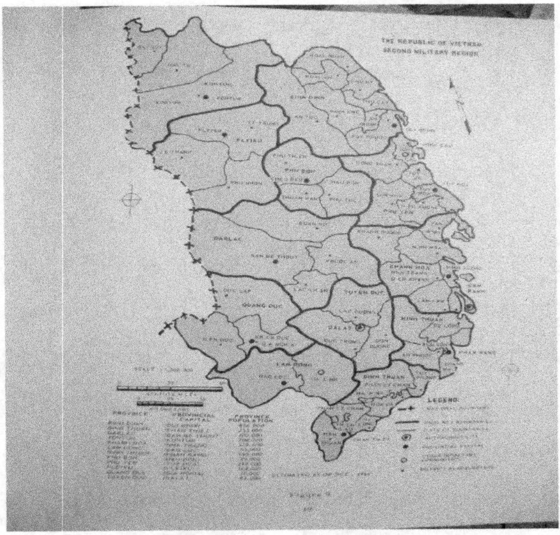

Figure 4: Map of II Corps

## *Division into Corps*

Vietnam was divided into five sections. I Corps was located to the north; II Corps was located in the Central Highlands, III Corps Central Delta areas, IV Corps in the Delta, and V Corps at the most southwestern part of the country.

Each of these areas had unique developments and was diversified among culture, tribes, villagers, and agriculture. There was little industry at this time in the country. Rice was the main crop in many areas. Bananas, Coconuts, Fish, and wild game supported the villages as well as chickens, goats, and pigs. Water Buffalo were the work horses for the farmers, as there were few tractors and farm equipment. There were weekly farmer's markets where fresh goods are purchased and sold. Water was a problem in regard to sanitation, as purification was questionable. Troops were supplied with water purification tablets to make the drinking water potable. Sewage systems were primitive or did not exist. The villages had an odor that you never forget. Many villager's businesses were small stores, restaurants, bars, and general stores. Refrigeration was done in sporadic increments due to the electrical shortages. Electricity would run about four hours a day and the food would have a period of time in the refrigerator relying on the insulation to keep them cool. Generators provided much of the electricity. Communication was sparse. There were few telephones, and no television. Local papers and pamphlets were the means for which information was shared.

The people used scooters, bicycles, and mopeds to travel, with few automobiles and trucks. Commercial trucks were small and resembled the trucks of Japan. They were overhead cabs over a small frame. Gasoline stations were scarce. The roads were narrow, and in many cases in poor condition. Mines were often in the roads and hindered transportation. Bridges were a target to be destroyed, both by the Air Force (Allies) and the VC to deter and stop movement. Highways were easy ambush targets, and travelers and convoys often were stopped and harassed. Check points were established by the US and Allies on the highways to ensure travelers had the “right papers” or documents and were not Viet Cong or NVA.

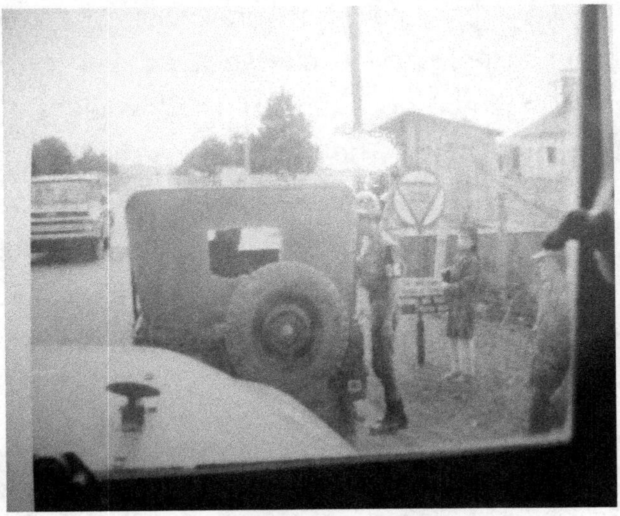

*Figure 5 Checkpoint*

The Central Highlands were mountainous, with large valleys in between. It was difficult to travel through them. The jungles were full of vegetation and triple canopy trees. There were dangers at every turn. Cobra snakes, bamboo vipers (the deadliest snake in the region) and many other wildlife inhabited the jungles. The chatter of monkeys could be heard nightly along with many species of insects and birds. Tigers and other carnivorous creatures roamed the countryside. Rats as big as housecats (Jungle Rats) were prevalent. Of course, it rained often, causing jungle rot on soldiers (Large red spots that seeped and covered the legs). To combat the dense vegetation and triple canopy jungle trees, the US government sprayed chemicals from airplanes to deter the growth. This was referred to as Agent Orange. Highway 19 was the main artery of East/ West travel from the Gulf of Tonkin (Que Nhon City) to Pleiku City and beyond to the Cambodian border in II Corp. In certain areas, elephants were used as a method of transportation.

Each village had their local provincial government. They would collect taxes, provide city services, and be a contact point for the national government. They would set the local laws and enforce them. The ARVN (Army of the Republic of Vietnam) would draft villagers by day to replenish their troops. At night, the Viet Cong did the same thing, only much more forcibly (Firsthand discussions with villagers confirmed that the VC would force at gunpoint young sons of the village to become a recruit.).

## Dissatisfaction with the War Effort

The draft was one way the U.S. troops were replenished. As more troops were needed, the draft increased the numbers. This was very unpopular and contributed to a growing dissent of the war. Demonstrations against the war were growing. Our government believed that more troops were needed to combat the strengthening enemy forces. A troop surge was requested by the Military, and over 500,000 troops were sent during this period to stop the insurgency. Many of us had the idealism to believe that the government was doing the right thing in a country far from home, and there was a duty to serve. However, U.S. citizens were not rationed, nor were they expected to sacrifice for the war effort. There was a conflict between the Doves and the Hawks in Congress. It caused bitterness, and unresolved differences. The war effort though was bipartisan starting under a Democratic President (John F. Kennedy) and ending under a Republican President (Gerald Ford). Four Presidents presided during this war. President Eisenhower only presided over advisors and was not a part of the war effort.

The anti-war effort began with persons outside of the mainstream. They were the "hippies," the out of work, the unemployables, students, and liberal academic teachers and professors. On the college campuses, the nickname for the student protestors were "green baggers," named for the green backpacks they usually carried. At first the demonstrations were in smaller groups, with homemade signs. It was truly a grass roots movement. Yet as the war continued, more people joined from the mainstream, asking Congress to end the war.

The military leaders planned military tactics and strategies. Their recommendation was always to conduct a war and to "win." I was one to support the military and believed that this was a stand to support democracy and stop the Communist movement. I joined the military despite all the fanfare against the war. Those of us that joined, whether voluntarily or drafted, put politics and our own desires aside to support the military and the war effort.

## *All of us are Grey Feathers*

A Grey feather is given to Indian Braves for every feat that they accomplished as they were growing up in the tribe. It was the first mark of distinction and showed that they were "selected" to represent the tribe in warfare, hunting, and fishing. Everyone was the same rank as another. They were sworn to protect each other, and to protect the tribe. When significant accomplishments occurred, a colored feather was given.

This philosophy of the Native American followed into the Vietnam War. All were "Braves" sworn to uphold the Constitution, and to serve and protect. It was an unwritten rule to "watch each other's back" and to work as a unit when engaged with an enemy force. The bravery and determination shown by all soldiers fighting in the war was led by "love of country" and that all of us wanted to become the best of the best and beat the enemy. It was a driver that most followed while serving in the Army. All of us earned the grey feather for completion of our service in that country.

*Figure 6 Indian Council giving out awards*

The draft served as a recruiting tool. The attitude was our own. Even those drafted developed the attitude to succeed and to become good soldiers. It was not what anyone wanted to do, but it was a duty. There was as much diversity in our ranks as there were soldiers. Some did not have formal education. Others graduated from college. Still others came from business. There was a myriad of reasons to join.

Those that did not choose to serve had deferments available to them—marriage, higher education, defense work, and hardship. However, the military was also an option to them, and some decided to forego the deferment and join. It was a duty some said and others an obligation to serve the country. They were Americans first and felt the need to serve. This created a unique mix of people in all of the services. It produced a camaraderie that few understood and created a feeling of belonging. It was a "watch your back and I will watch yours" philosophy.

# 3$^{RD}$ Battalion, 12$^{TH}$ Infantry, 4$^{TH}$ Infantry Division

During the period of 1967 through 1970 the 3$^{rd}$ Battalion 12$^{th}$ Infantry, 4$^{th}$ Infantry Division fought gallantly against a hostile force that was heavily armed and well organized to fight against South Vietnam and its Allies (U. S and the West). They were supported by roads that could manage heavy equipment. They had no significant air power available to them. In this period an average of 80 to 120 United States soldiers per week lost their lives in various areas of the countryside. Fighting did not happen every day, but patrols were on-going. The synopsis of the actions directly affected the overall feeling of common goals and fostered the feeling of all helping each other. Through the common associations in the realm of fire, each soldier earned the grey feather.

This story describes the events in II Corps where 3d Battalion, 12$^{th}$ Infantry had their operations. II Corps was a mountainous area with many hills, and mountains in the area. Hills were usually named by the meters above sea level. The range of height of the hills and mountains were from 500 meters above sea level to over 2000 meters. The valleys were used for planting rice and other crops as well as harboring water buffalo and farm animals. There often was a mist surrounding the mountains in the morning as well as fog. Monsoons were heaviest in the summer. Once in a while a storm caused from Typhoons would play havoc with the troops. The rains were extremely heavy, and mudslides did occur. Resupply efforts were often cancelled until a later date due to the fog and poor visibility.

The language barrier hindered communication by the U.S. troops to the local villagers, preventing information from being shared. However, pictures were drawn, and the villagers were as helpful as they could be under the circumstances.

From all of this the troops would arrive in Vietnam by air into an air base near Bien Hoa, Hue, or Cam Ran Bay. The air bases were staging areas where troops would get their clothing, weapons, and supplies in preparation for movement to their duty base camp. There was an orientation for all troops as to what to expect, first aid review, and strategic discussions.

RF soldiers learn their trade
Story on page 10

*Figure 7 Training Troops for New Arrivals in-Country*

After two days, the troops were moved by Caribous (C130's) to the airbases in their area. It was not easy to leave wives, girlfriends, friends, family, work, and the "world as they knew it." The only news was in a paper called the "Stars and Stripes" or the magazine "Espirit" and that was mostly about the war efforts. Music was by tape and played at the base camps.

Radio programs were scripted and taped. Few soldiers had access, but when they did it was listened to. The radio programs would always greet the troops with “Good Morning Vietnam.” It sounded strange but was well received. Yet the world events and events within the U.S. were unknown. We were living in a vacuum of news and sometimes of our families. The mail was “free” for soldiers to send to the US, but slow. Telephone lines to the “world” were scarce, and the wait was long. At times packages were sent to the troops, and these were shared by all. It was appreciated.

The travel from Bien Hoa to the II Corps base camp was a world apart. Bien Hoa was in a safe area, where there were few instances of insurgency. II Corps had many sightings that included both North Vietnamese (NVA) soldiers and Viet Cong (VC). NVA soldiers were units of the North Vietnamese Army that infiltrated the country by way of Cambodia and Laos, by ocean, and by the roads going through the country. The Viet Cong were insurgents who lived in the villages and functioned as a day worker in retail, farm, or restaurant/bar and a soldier at night. They disliked the South Vietnam government and their policies, and even some disdain for the country’s religions. They did not like foreign intervention, and they had little respect for the local governments and leaders. They were true guerrilla fighters and would engage and withdraw without detection. To counteract the VC and the NVA, the South Vietnamese formed ARVN (Army Republic of Vietnam) regiments, who often operated independently, and had their own objectives. U.S. advisors would be in the units to help them develop combat tactics, use weapons properly, and to assist in getting them stronger. They were part of MAC-V (Military Army Command

Vietnam) and placed in the II Corp as well. Special Forces units were stationed in outlying areas to provide reconnaissance and first response if needed. In addition, there were many support elements—helicopter pilots and warrant officers, supply personnel, quartermaster areas, transportation hubs, medical facilities, mess tents and cooks, administration areas, mortar platoons, artillery regiments, air force bases, naval weapons areas, signal corps individuals, and combat engineering troops. There was danger at every point. Women served as nurses, as Red Cross workers, as administrators during the conflict. They too had a large part that was important to the operation. All served with the highest recognition.

While the size of units is classified, it is important to give a perspective as to approximate sizes of force. A squad is usually 4-8 men, plus a squad leader. A platoon ranges from 20 to 30 in the field, but often is less under combat conditions. There are usually 4 platoons plus a mortar unit in a company. An artillery unit may also be attached to a battalion. There are usually 4 to 5 companies plus a headquarters company to make up a battalion. There may also be battalion trains areas with additional personnel. In the field companies may average 100 men, and battalions about 800. On the enemy side, a company–size force is about 100 men. A regiment-size force is about 500. A division size is about 5000. Different conflicts will drastically change these numbers. They do give a point of reference to help better understand the actions and confrontations.

# CHAPTER TWO 1967 OPERATIONS

## *Dak To Province 1967*

From countless patrols in a region harassed by Viet Cong hit and run tactics, booby traps, and villager kidnappings, my unit was constantly on alert. However, there were few incidents of combat activity. All foot soldiers had nicknames or were referred to by their last names as they sloshed through rice paddies, trudged up and down hills and mountains, and searched for an enemy that hid in the daylight, and harassed at night. When they did confront us in the daylight, they would hit us with small arms and rockets, and immediately run away to make pursuit of them difficult, even with aircraft helping with searches. Our day began early. We called it early morning rough it, as it was militarily referred to as EMNT or early morning nautical time. It was the time when some light peaked through the night sky, giving some light to see the trails. While on military maneuvers hills were referred to by meters high from sea level. However, we decided to name the hills rather than call them out by the number. Hill 550 may be referred to Coconut Hill. This added some color and excitement to the dullness of patrolling through dense jungle growth.

Reading a map was exceedingly difficult, especially among the mountain ranges. Maps were topographical, and sometimes misinterpreted. Combat platoon leaders were the main readers of the map and directed their platoon and squads in the direction to follow. Most of the time the movement from one point to another was completed. Once in a while though the terrain was more difficult to read due to dense vegetation and height of the hill or mountain. Monsoon rains sometimes blurred the map since most of the time it was not in a plastic container during movement. The soldiers had a nickname for this as well stating, "the most dangerous thing in the Army was a 2$^{nd}$ Lieutenant with a map and compass". But all kidding aside, all helped the platoon leader keep on track. It was hazardous when the platoon was not following the map and off course.

The dangers of the jungle have often been displayed by Walt Disney and Movies, but most of that hype was not true. We rarely saw snakes, tigers, or elephants in the jungle. We did see many monkeys who often followed us in the tree. At night jungle rats would patrol around our patrol base. Some were as large as a house cat. The real danger, however, was the enemy that walked among us, then hit us when we least expected it. They would always either hit the point element first, and withdraw quickly into the tree line, or they would hit the small element in the back who were concentrating on their forward movement, and not paying as much attention to the back of them. Other things that occurred involved the men who smoked at night. The VC would wait until a match was lit and fire into our patrol base.

On May 1$^{st}$, 1967, intelligence through the 3rd Brigade Commander warned the battalion commander 3$^{rd}$ Battalion, 12$^{th}$ Infantry that two NVA companies were moving toward Company A's perimeter. The company was advised to prepare for an imminent attack and stay in position. Patrols were sent out to determine the strength, direction, and size of the hostile unit(s).

*Figure 8 Dak To Mountains and surrounding area*

Company A was airlifted into the area northwest of Dak To. It was to search for NVA (North Vietnam Army) presence in that locality. Dak To was being harassed nightly by 122mm rockets over the past month, and an unfriendly force was detected. Company A set up their perimeter and began sending out patrols to sweep the area around the patrol base.

One patrol found a telephone wire along the trail leading to the company's perimeter. The patrol cut the wire and reported it to the commander. A few minutes' later four men at a listening post reported observing 30 to 40 NVA soldiers moving toward them. The conversation between the listening post and the company commander is below.

"Alpha 6 this is Lima Papa 1 ( LP1), we spot 30 NVA coming right towards you," said the listening post. 6 is the code name for the company commander of Company A. LP1 is the listening post, consisting of four men, placed as an observation post. There were usually four listening posts that set up around a defensive position to cover all directions. Each one was numbered. Likewise, each platoon leader was numbered, as well as each squad leader.

"LP1 this is 6, over," said the Company A commander.

"6 this is LP1," said the listening post.

"Blow your claymores, and move quickly back to the base," said the A Company Commander.

"Roger that," said the listening post.

The listening post blew their claymore mines, and hurriedly moved to the perimeter. Not far behind them were the NVA soldiers, who pursued them. They just made it into the perimeter and immediately sought cover (digging a hole to protect them from incoming fire or seeking other cover). It was now 0645 hours.

At 0700 hours an estimated NVA company (100 men) attacked the perimeter from the Southeast. The first platoon received heavy automatic weapons fire, B-40 rockets, and mortars.

"1(Platoon Leader of the first platoon) this is 6, over," said the Company Commander.

"6 go ahead," said the 1st platoon leader.

"Direct artillery 200 meters and direct fire," said 6.

"Roger that," said the first platoon leader, and began directing artillery fire into the oncoming NVA soldiers.

Artillery fire was placed around the perimeter and airstrikes were requested to suppress enemy fire.

"Cobra 1, from Smoke on the ground direct fire to the Southeast," said the A Company Commander to the helicopter gunship.

"Roger that, ETA (Estimated time of arrival) 5 minutes," said Cobra 1.

At this point only light casualties had been sustained by the company and small arms fire against their positions began to subside, although 82 mm mortars continued to fall within their perimeter. While the men began to breathe easier with the attack from the southeast subsiding, a sudden attack by a platoon-sized force (30 men) from the Southwest side occurred with an intense volume of small arms fire, mortars, and rockets. The listening post (LP2) was overrun first and then the NVA soldiers attacked the main perimeter. A sapper (NVA sapper had a long pole filled with explosives.) unit was sent in to make a path for attacking soldiers. The perimeter was breached and hand to hand combat ensued along with close in shots from their AK47's. The men of Company A fought back gallantly. Radio contact was lost. The company commander could not communicate to his commanders to request external artillery and air support. Ammunition was getting low

"1 this is 6, redirect mortar fire to the Southwest, about 150 meters out," said 6.

"6 this is 1, can't switch quickly. Mortars hit within the perimeter and damaged guns. Will work as quickly as I can," said the first platoon leader. Meanwhile the fight continued within the perimeter. Finally, radio communication was reinstated, and the company commander bravely called for Artillery and helicopter gunship support.

Within ten minutes fire was directed within the perimeter against the hostile force. It forced them to withdraw, but not without casualties. Due to the great amount of artillery and airstrikes hitting the perimeter the NVA did not flee and instead "hugged" the US perimeter in the thick underbrush. These forces were a delaying force to cover the main attack element as the enemy withdrew carrying their dead and wounded. Personnel in the perimeter received intense small arms fire when any attempt was made to move. Artillery was shifted to block avenues of escape. Patrols went in pursuit of the withdrawing enemy, but contact could not be reestablished. Sweeps around the perimeter located 24 NVA bodies and one wounded NVA soldier who was captured. The weapons and equipment found on the enemy contact site confirmed the well-equipped status of the NVA in the Central highlands. Company A had three soldiers killed in action (KIA) and fourteen wounded in action (WIA).

From May 2nd to May 20th the unit conducted a search and destroy mission along the Cambodian border that was west of "Jackson Hole." Most of the villagers had abandoned the area during this search. The terrain was rugged, and the undergrowth was thick, and difficult to maneuver during patrols. Each unit on maneuvers typically went down trails in a single file. The point element was most important as they were the first to detect traps or hostile units ahead. There were signs of NVA units operating in the area. However, there was not any activity or sightings during the patrols.

*Figure 9 NVA Weapons Cache Found*

Several weapons' caches were found where the NVA stored mortar rounds, and other ammunition. When found, the platoons destroyed them. The valley was also searched for food supplies and local inhabitants who may be aiding the NVA. It was reported through ARVN units in the area that sounds of heavy truck movement during the night hours, and the sound of men moving along the trails could be heard. One sighting included a Russian helicopter dropping supplies to a NVA unit. That was never confirmed. The trail itself was referred to as Ho Chi Minh trail, named after the leader of North Vietnam. The trail was one of the infiltration routes used by the North Vietnamese to enter South Vietnam. It was universally used throughout the war for coming and going. It also was a main supply route for the NVA.

On May 20th, the battalion began operations north of the Chu Kram Mountains to block the infiltration routes. On May 21st Company B was moved by helicopter and arrived at their night location at 1600 hours. Suddenly the NVA began to drop mortar rounds and B-40 rockets within their perimeter. Artillery was adjusted on the suspected hostile positions. Within minutes after the artillery barrage began, the company perimeter received a ground attack from the north, northeast, and northwest. A force of 100 NVA soldiers stormed toward the company size perimeter and attempted to overrun it.

Company C which was located 1000 meters east was directed to move as rapidly as possible to reinforce Company B's position. As Company C arrived another ground attack ensued, supported with mortars and rockets. They moved to within 25 meters of the Company C perimeter. The Company C commander called in artillery to direct fire on the NVA position. The incoming rounds were accurately placed on the attacking elements. With the added fire support from the artillery battery, the NVA attack was stopped. They withdrew from the perimeter and evacuated the area.

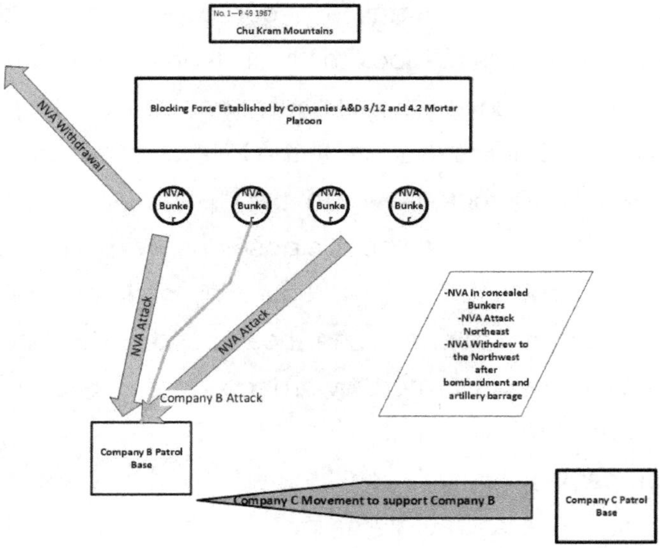


*Schematic Drawing 1—Chu Kram Mountains*

"1 and 2, this is 6, over." Said the C Company Commander

"This is 1." "This is 2." Said the two platoon leaders of the first and second platoon.

"1 move NE, 2 move NW in pursuit," said the C Company Commander (6).

"Roger that," said the platoon leaders.

The Battalion commander directed the two platoons to pursue the hostile force, supported by artillery fire to their front. The two platoons conducted a limited pursuit due to the lateness of the day and the dense undergrowth which made an extensive search too dangerous and difficult.

"6 this is 1. It is 1930 hours, and we cannot see the trails. No signs of NVA. Coming back in." Shortly afterward, 2 repeated the same message.

"Roger that," said 6.

"MedEvac have wounded and dead. Need transport. Smoke is on the field." said the C Company Commander.

"6, this is Medevac 21, on the way. See smoke," said the helicopter pilot.

The Medevac landed in a field close by the perimeter. Flares were sent up to light up the landing zone. The platoons quickly placed their wounded on the chopper and prepared their dead by placing them in body bags for transport. Sniper fire directed at the Medevac missed as it left the LZ.

The results of the attack were four US soldiers killed in action (KIA) and seventeen wounded in action (WIA).

The next day a search was conducted around the perimeter and found that the NVA lost 37 men killed. One NVA soldier was wounded and left on the battlefield. He was captured and questioned. From the captured soldier, he indicated it was a NVA company (about 100 men in strength) that attacked the perimeter. It was a part of a NVA regiment (about 500 men) in the area. He believed the direction of the enemy was to enter Cambodia and recoup their losses. The captured soldier was removed and taken by helicopter back to the brigade base for further questioning and confined, under the guidelines of the Geneva Convention. The NVA unit left behind a squad to hinder operations from pursuit, but quickly they withdrew to join the remainder of the NVA unit. No other incidents occurred that day. The equipment recovered from them included six individual weapons (6 AK-47 rifles and 1 magazine) and two crew-served weapons.

From June 23$^{rd}$ to August 16$^{th}$ 1967, the battalion headquarters was moved to "Jackson Hole". The 3$^{rd}$ Battalion 12$^{th}$ Infantry commenced blocking operations west of that location. There were only a few incidents that occurred during that time. It gave the battalion time to get new troops on board, conduct training, and prepare for the next operation. Camp Enari was used for the training, and companies rotated themselves in and out of Camp Enari near Pleiku.

On August 17th, the battalion began operations east of Plei Djereng and north of highway 509. The battalion pushed to the northeast from the highway until September 2nd. There was only one incident in this period for Company C when they came upon a NVA campsite. They quickly returned fire and overrun the camp, leaving one NVA soldier killed in action.

From September 3rd to October 11th the battalion conducted operations with the 2nd brigade. The operations were conducted in "VC Valley," a recognized stronghold for the Viet Cong. The valley was just east of Camp Enari. The search for Viet Cong found many huts and storage areas where the VC stored their supplies. Villagers were questioned as to Viet Cong activities, but no added information was received. There were several instances where the huts (called hooches) were booby trapped with hand grenades (Chi-Com Grenades). Pungi sticks (small sticks with pointed ends, some poisoned) were found along the trail, and animal traps were placed in areas along a trail to entrap soldiers. The pits were lined with sharpened points to maim the soldiers. However, no significant contacts occurred, just some sporadic sniper fire. The unit returned to Camp Enari. The battalion was then moved to the ***Plei Djereng*** area at LZ (Landing Zone) Three Tango. A search and destroy mission were conducted to locate arms caches and possible NVA units. This time there were no significant findings.

# Ngok Tang Mountains—Operation MacArthur

On November 1st, the battalion was moved to Dak To province in the Ngok Tang Mountain range to start the offensive phase of Operation MacArthur. The operation was conducted from November 3rd to November 11th.

On November 3rd Company A and Company B were transported by helicopter into the Ngok Tang Mountains. The lead element received heavy sniper fire as they moved from the landing zone to their designated night location. The small arms fire became stronger as the company returned fire and began an assault toward their positions.

"Alpha 6, this is Alpha 1. There is heavy incoming fire at LZ (Landing Zone). Moving to outside of LZ and returning fire. Need artillery directed around the LZ zone. Pinned down at location and not able to move forward," said the first platoon leader.

"1, this is 6. Roger that. Artillery is on the way. Choppers called in gun ship support. Helicopter gunners directing fire on perimeter. Keep firing and move off the LZ. Seek cover. Throw smoke at your position," said the Company Commander.

Artillery was called to direct fire on the NVA positions. Another assault was waged, only to be held back due the heavily fortified positions that were camouflaged. The NVA planned their cover well, and had dug into the hillside deeply, concealing all fortified positions. In fact, if you did not know they were there, you could not see them. Heavy rocks and sod hid each bunker position. The estimated hostile force was company size or about 100 men.

"6, this is 1. See bunkers, heavy machine gun fire directed at us. Request return back to LZ," said the first platoon leader.

"1 this is 6, Permission granted," said the Company Commander.

Companies A and B withdrew to permit an airstrike with high explosives. Phantom F4 fighter jets swarmed the sky above them, dropping 300 lb. bombs at the suspected bunker locations. Artillery rounds were also directed at them by the forward observers located near the bunkers. Later that afternoon the two companies set up camp at an old American perimeter just below the NVA trench system. Airstrikes and artillery continued throughout the night. On November 4$^{th}$ Company B again moved toward them. The lead element left at 0830 hours. They immediately received automatic weapons fire, sniper fire, and mortars. More airstrikes were requested. At 1130 hours, Company B began to move against the opponent once again. The two lead platoons from the company were cut off from the intense automatic weapons fire and mortars. The platoons returned fire and withdrew back to the perimeter. Two men were missing in action (MIA), and 24 men were wounded in action (WIA). The companies withdrew to the LZ (landing zone) to set up a night position while artillery and airstrikes pounded the hostile positions for eighteen continuous hours.

On Sunday November 5$^{th}$ Company A moved up the mountain, encountering only sporadic sniper fire. They searched the area and found twenty-seven NVA soldiers killed in action, laying in bunkers and trenches. There were numerous drag marks, blood stains, and flesh embedded in tree bark that indicated that a higher toll of enemy had been taken.

Companies C and D were airlifted to the Battalion firebase on the northeast side of Ngok Tang in the afternoon of November 9th. They contacted a company-size unit (100 NVA) on Cobra Hill and withdrew to their perimeter to call in airstrikes and artillery on the positions. On the following morning they conducted an on-line assault up Cobra Hill. The move up the hill was exceedingly difficult due to sniper fire from the top of the hill, and incoming mortars hitting the columns moving forward. Finally, the top of Cobra Hill was reached. The NVA attempted to engage us by small arms fire, RPG (Rifle Propelled Grenades), B-40 rockets, and automatic weapons. Each time they fired, we returned fire. The men responded gallantly with bullets flying over their heads and averting shrapnel from the incoming mortar fire. Finally, they were able to stop the incoming rounds. The NVA withdrew hurriedly down the opposite side of the hill. A search of the contact site found one 60 mm mortar tube and several rounds of munitions, 3 AK-47 rifles, and several documents that were left behind. The victory was not without casualties, as Company C suffered the loss of ten men killed in action (KIA) and 24 men wounded (WIA). Eleven NVA soldiers were found Killed.

On November 11th, the companies moved west from Cobra Hill to a suspected NVA position on Bamboo Hill. Enemy snipers and automatic weapons stopped the movement just below the crest of the hill. Airstrikes and artillery were called in to support the troop movement. After the bombs pounded the hill throughout the afternoon, two platoons worked their way to the top of the hill to search the area and make a reconnaissance of the area. However, a well-entrenched force engaged them in a fierce battle. The NVA Company was located in trenches and bunkers. At 1830 hours the battle ended, and the platoons returned back to the company perimeter. The NVA were observed withdrawing to the North. There were many casualties received during the attack. Three men were killed in action and eleven were wounded. The NVA had 13 dead. Bamboo Hill was also seized that day.

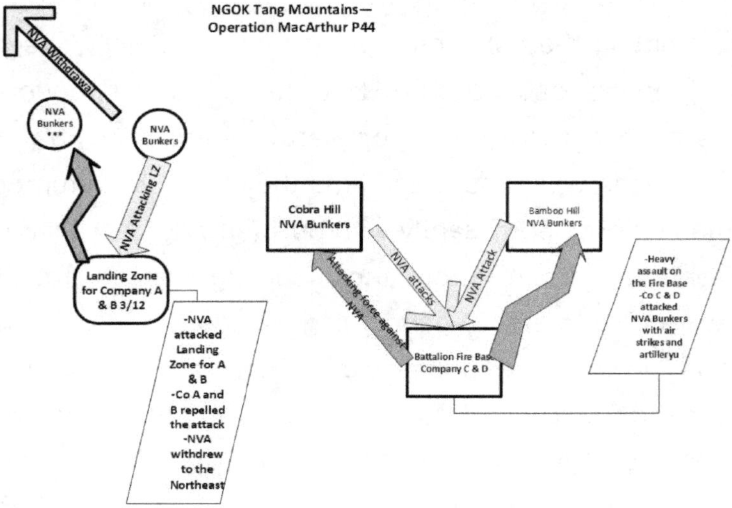


*Schematic Drawing 2—NGOK Tang Mountains*

Snoopy the Red Baron was called to their location to reconnaissance the area and lay down devastating fire on the withdrawing NVA. The plane was an old, converted Douglas AC-47 Spooky (also nicknamed "Puff, the Magic Dragon") It was the first in a series of fixed-wing gunships developed by the United States Air Force during the Vietnam War. It was designed to provide more firepower than light and medium ground-attack aircraft in certain situations when ground forces called for close air support.

*Figure 10 Snoopy the Red Baron Gunship*

Company D and A were moved east along the ridgeline. There was no further contact with the NVA unit until November $16^{th}$. The pursuit phase of the operation began. Companies A, C, and the Reconnaissance platoon maneuvered troops up the slopes of Shadow Box Hill. On November $16^{th,}$ a platoon from Company C contacted an unknown enemy force in a trench and bunker complex on the approach to Shadow Box Hill. The patrol withdrew and called artillery and airstrikes on the NVA positions. At 0800 hours on November $17^{th}$ Company A linked up with Company C and the Reconnaissance platoon. They began their assault at 0815 hours. They were engaged less than 200 meters from where they started moving forward. The estimated enemy size was a battalion fully entrenched in bunkers, trenches, and tunnels. Company A and C withdrew back to their perimeter and called for artillery and air strikes on the enemy positions. FO's (Forward observers) positioned themselves less than 50 meters from the dug-in positions to direct the air attack and artillery fire. They are individual soldiers who position themselves close to NVA locations to direct fire and provide tactical information to the companies and platoons. At times they may be placed in low flying aircraft to direct airstrikes. These planes were referred to as the "Pregnant Pelican" as they had glass fronts for the observers to have an unobstructed view of the area. Their slow speed enabled better observation to direct air strikes and artillery on enemy positions.

*Figure 11 Observation Plane ("Pregnant Pelican") with Glass Front.*

At 1130 hours the attack began again toward objective Shadow Box Hill. Again, intense fire from small arms, machine guns, mortar rounds, and B-40 rockets halted their movement forward. Airstrikes and artillery again directed fire on them. At 1430 hours the infantry unit began again to move up the hill. It was treacherous and painfully slow. The platoons maneuvered under a continuous fusillade of automatic weapons, mortars, B-40 rockets, and sniper fire. At 1800 hours after ten hours of continuous battle, the two companies and reconnaissance platoon secured Shadow Box Hill. Nine soldiers were killed in Action and thirty-two soldiers were wounded in action. The reconnaissance platoon searched the area and found over sixty NVA dead, with numerous blood trails leading off the southern slopes of the hill. Also found was a complex series of trenches, bunkers, and tunnels that was one of the largest finds of the conflict, including medical supplies and an operating room.

On November 18th Company B was airlifted from Lion Hill to Cobra Hill to support search and destroy missions from that location. The next day in the afternoon Company B conducted an attack on Shadow Box Hill where they contacted an unknown-size force. The company withdrew and set up a night perimeter. Artillery and airstrikes directed fire on that location throughout the night. The next morning Company B conducted a search of the hill without incident. They had withdrawn. Seven NVA bodies were found at the top of the hill. Both A and B conducted searches until November 23rd of Cobra and Shadow Box Hills as well as their surroundings without any significant contact.

Company A and Company B moved by helicopter to Lion Hill to prepare a mortar base to support subsequent operations on Viper Hill further west. Early in the afternoon on November 25th, the companies received five rounds of 82mm mortar fire. Light casualties resulted from the attack.

On November 26th, Company B and Company C moved from Lion Hill to Viper Hill where Company B discovered a 122 mm rocket position and assorted items of rocket equipment and containers. Several NVA bodies were found as preparations continued on the new battalion firebase. On November 30th while the battalion commander was doing a reconnaissance flight, the helicopter received 12.7 mm Anti-aircraft fire. Fortunately, it missed the target. However, this confirmed the reports that anti-aircraft weapons were being utilized by the NVA in the Dak To area of operations.

Throughout the month of December, the battalion continued to conduct search and destroy operations to the west toward the Cambodian border. On December 2nd Company B and Company C encountered an unknown size enemy force west of the Battalion firebase. The companies were able to withdraw and direct artillery and airstrikes on the positions for two consecutive days. On December 4th, the two companies moved into the hostile locations without contact. On December 24th Company C engaged an estimated company-sized force (about 100 NVA) in the early afternoon and withdrew to a company perimeter while airstrikes and artillery struck at their positions. That night the company perimeter received numerous rounds of mortar fire. By morning, the mortar fire ended, as the enemy withdrew from the area. Searches of the area revealed no NVA movement or presence.

# CHAPTER THREE TET 1968

For the first three weeks of January, the Battalion returned back to "Jackson Hole" to stand down and replenish its troops. New troops were being trained at Camp Enari, outside of Pleiku City. Equipment was refurbished, maintenance was provided to trucks and weapons; mortar supplies were replenished, and training was conducted for future operations. Hot meals and showers, a bed, and shelter were provided. There were also recreational activities at the base to help the troops unwind from the rigors of combat.

The commanders reviewed the lessons learned from each contact that occurred and reviewed future intelligence reports. Tactics and strategies were discussed as to what was successful, and what needed to be improved. Troop morale in the field was also of importance to discuss. Other discussions included the orientation and incorporation into the unit of new platoon leaders, new Non-commissioned officers, and new recruits. The goal was to make them effective the minute they go to the combat unit The circumstances surrounding soldiers who were declared missing in action were reviewed by the staff. A thorough set of interviews with all who were involved was conducted. Once this was completed, a report of the findings was forwarded to the chain of command. Some of the missing may have been captured and become prisoners of war. Others were casualties that were not retrieved when the combat ended. It was important to determine each man's fate. The objective of this investigation and detailed reporting had only one mission—to find them and bring them home.

Each troop replenished their "C" rations to take into the field. "C" rations were canned goods, and each troop received 14 cartons of them to place in their ruck sacks. Also, the troops received the most valuable tool in their ruck sack—the can opener. They also received two bars of C-4, an explosive when attached with a fuse. C-4 was used to cook the "C" rations in the field. It was not explosive until the fuse was attached and lit. The flame of the C-4 was hot and reduced the cooking time. The most hated can of all was ham and lima beans. Chicken noodle, beef, canned fruit, pound cake, cheddar cheese, and crackers were the most favorite. Pizza was made by applying cheddar cheese on a cracker, then topping it with tabasco sauce. The tabasco sauce was one item the soldiers purchased while back in base camp. It was like gold to them. When all fourteen days of rations were placed in the ruck sack as well as the jungle blanket and poncho, the weight approached 90 pounds. Often there was trading among the troops, and items such as ham and lima beans were discarded. The troops would rather starve than eat that. Water tablets were given for the troops to purify their water in their canteens while on maneuvers. Malaria tablets were required daily. Salt tablets were also issued to the troops to protect against heat exhaustion. The troops had newly washed clothes, hot food, showers, and now new rations and were now prepared to go. Of course, ammunition supplies were replenished as well.

By the end of three weeks, the troops were ready and prepared for the next operations. Helicopters were combat assaulted to Firebase 25 formerly an abandoned fire base.

It was located northwest of the village of Dak To, which was about 40 kilometers northwest of Pleiku city. The movements occurred on January 17th and 18th, 1968.

Landing Zone on Combat Assault

*Figure 12 Combat Assault into Firebase 25*

## Nob Hill

At 0845 hours on January 19, 1968, Company B, 3d Battalion, 12th Infantry departed fire support base 25 on a search and clear 6 Kilometers northwest of firebase 25 to locate a NVA platoon size force (about 25 men) spotted on Nob Hill. Company B had been moving northwest when the point element spotted an enemy soldier 200 meters from their position 2 kilometers from the objective.

"TOC (Tactical Operations Center), this is 6 Bravo, request fire 200 SE of Nob Hill," said the company commander of Company B.

"Fire in the hole, direct, over," stated TOC radio operator.

"Roger that, see first hit, move 30 meters Whiskey (West), fire for effect."

Mortar fire was called for and directed but the enemy soldier fled in a Northwest direction. The mortars continued for the next hour, surrounding the area with mortar rounds.

The NVA avoided the impacting rounds and began to move back toward Company B's location. They quickly and stealthily used the thick underbrush to their advantage, since they could not be spotted from the air. They set up an ambush along the trail Company B was traveling. They split up into three units, with one being the blocking force on the trail, and the other two on each side of the trail. Ambush mines were put in place as well as automatic weapon positions. Snipers climbed trees to conceal themselves. Since the movement was undetected Company B continued moving toward the ambush positions. The point element detected movement about 50 meters from them at 1217 hours, but it was too late.

At 1221 hours Company B was ambushed in the vicinity of Nob Hill by a sudden attack by an estimated 60 NVA soldiers from three directions. The platoon-size force was underestimated, and now it was a company size or larger of about 100 NVA. The fire and crossfires into the perimeter of Company B was intense. Automatic weapon fire was also directed on the unit. They were expecting our arrival and were able to inflict immediate casualties.

"TOC (Tactical Operations Center, and usually includes command staff, artillery unit, supply and mess plus main resupply landing zone), this is 6 Bravo. We are getting hit. We have casualties. There is a large force on three sides of the trail. Over," said the Company B Commander.

"Roger that, what is your LQ (Lima Quebec or meaning Location)?" said the Battalion Commander.

"We are at the base of Nob Hill, need artillery support. Any choppers available?" said the Company B commander.

"Negative artillery battery support only. Will you direct, fire for effect?"

"Roger that, will direct," said 6 Bravo (Company B Commander).

The company commander directed his company into a perimeter and tried in vain to retrieve the wounded and dead. Because of the intense fire the enemy was deploying with small arms, automatic weapons, and Chi-Com grenades, the effort to recover the dead cost Company B additional casualties. Meanwhile, a platoon-size hostile force had worked its way around the hastily formed perimeter in an effort to surround company B and to cut it off from the fire support base. At 1335 hours company B received heavy mortar and rifle propelled grenades (RPG), resulting in more casualties, including the company commander.

"TOC (Tactical Operations Center) this is 1 Bravo. 6 Bravo is down. B-40 rockets being fired, Pinned down. MG (Machine gun) fire, RPG, and SA (Small arms) fire raking perimeter, over," said the 1st platoon leader who became the acting company commander.

"Fix Bayonets, and keep your machetes and grenades ready," said each of the platoon leaders to their men.

Company B fought gallantly against a large force. Surrounded and under intense fire, the platoon leaders directed them to seek cover and fire into the jungle areas, aiming at the snipers, and automatic weapon positions. The acting Company

Commander wanted a tight perimeter to get the most results from his overtaxed troops.

"1 Bravo this is TOC. Move 300 meters southeast. Set up perimeter. " said the battalion commander.

"Roger that TOC," said 1 Bravo.

"1 Bravo, artillery rounds fired for effect. Should go right over you," said TOC

Using the artillery rounds as a cover the 1st platoon leader directed Company B to move 300 meters southeast to allow room for more intense artillery and air support to hit the enemy. The artillery fire had insignificant effect on the NVA because they were so entrenched in the jungle undergrowth, it was difficult to direct fire and do damage to them. The move was difficult, with heavy sniper fire placed into the withdrawing column. Finally, Company B set up a perimeter at the specified location, 300 meters from Nob Hill.

"TOC, this is 1 Bravo. Cannot see rounds hit. Believe it to be on target. But we cannot see the enemy locations from here. Setting up perimeter now, "said the acting company commander (1st platoon leader).

"1 Bravo, this is TOC getting help from Charlie. Keep troops together and return fire. More to follow," said the battalion commander.

"This is 1 Bravo, Roger that, TOC," said 1st platoon leader, Company B.

At this point Company C departed the Fire support base 25 to eliminate the enemy blocking force and ambush positions to provide cover for Company B withdrawal. Company C, though, encountered heavy sniper fire from its flanks as it moved down the trail toward Company B's location. Company C was able to return fire against the sniper locations (located in the trees) and eliminate the danger.

"1 Bravo this is 6 Charlie. Moving toward your location. We are about 200 meters from you. Start moving toward us. Over," said Company C Commander.

"Roger that, 6 Charlie, this is 1 Bravo. 2, 3, 4 move out. 2nd platoons take lead," said 1st platoon leader, acting Company Commander Company B.

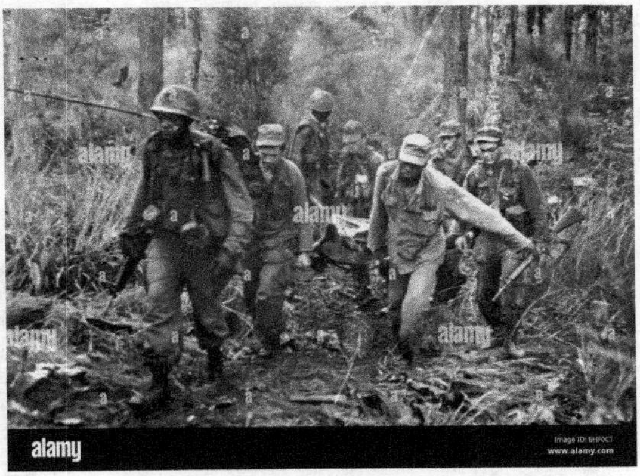


*Figure 13 Withdrawal and transporting wounded from battlefield*

The wounded and the dead were placed on litters or on ponchos and carried with them as they proceeded from their perimeter to Company C's location. Sniper fire and small arms fire continued to hamper the movement. At 1510 hours a Company C Listening post (LP) observed Company B coming into the perimeter.

"Charlie 6, this is Lima Papa 1 (Listening Post). Bravo here. Hold fire," said the listening post.

"Roger that," said the company commander. He issued the command to the company to hold their fire and allow Company B to enter.

Company B joined the perimeter of Company C. Once the two companies joined, they immediately started toward fire base 25 and returned at 1730. The withdrawal route to the fire support base was without further incident. The NVA withdrew to Nob Hill to regroup and retrench.

The results of the Company B encounter with a well-equipped and well-trained NVA force were one killed in action (KIA), four missing in action (MIA), and twenty-eight wounded in action (WIA). Company C had no casualties, but a forward observer attached to the unit was killed in action. Twenty-one NVA soldiers were killed in the action.

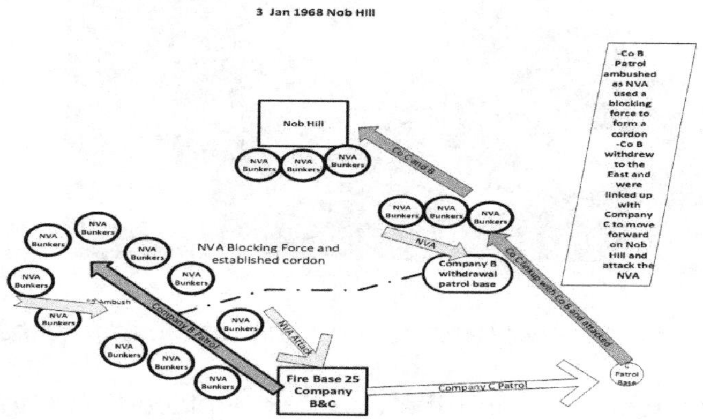


*Schematic Drawing 3—Nob Hill*

Artillery and mortars continued to pound the NVA location on Nob Hill. In addition, three tactical airstrikes (TAC AIR) were called on the location during the day. Phantom F4 jets were used for the bombing mission. They carried 250 lb. bombs.

*Figure 14 Phantom Jet (F4) Supporting Operations*

Two runs of HP (High explosive or phosphorous bombs) were also placed on the Nob Hill. The airplanes could not see any movement or any indication a NVA unit was still on it. However, on the third run, an anti-aircraft rocket was seen fired from there.

*Figure 15 B52 Bomber*

The Air Force Phantom F4 Pilots called to their base commander to move B-52 Bombers to bomb Nob Hill. The B-52 base commander mobilized a B-52 plane and directed it to bomb the hill. The nickname for this B52 plane was "Big Daddy." It was filled with 500 lb. bombs, and its effect was devastating. The bombs dropped in the early evening hours. The sounds were deafening and could be heard at the fire support base 25. Even the ground shook when they were dropped. The bombing continued for about an hour. When that ended "Snoopy" followed later that evening and started spraying the suspected enemy locations with bullets. (Snoopy was a converted C130 equipped with 50 Caliber Machine guns and other weaponry." The steady red stream of bullets could be seen from the fire support base. This continuous fire lasted two hours. The results of the barrage were unknown, but it is believed to have inflicted severe casualties on the withdrawing hostile forces. NVA movement to the northwest was detected as they withdrew.

The next day on January 20$^{th}$ at 0945 hours Company C departed Fire Support Base 25 in hopes of trying to locate the bodies of six soldiers who were missing in action from Company B and to also clear the ridge and hill of the contact site. In the meantime, the enemy soldiers had moved from the objective towards firebase 25. They were able to dig in along the trail where Company C was traveling and placed units on the flanks and the front in preparation for an ambush. Within seventeen minutes after departure Company C received extremely heavy fire from automatic weapons and small arms as well as hand grenades.

"TOC, this is 6 Charlie. Getting hit. Over," said the C Company Commander. In the meantime, C Company formed a defensive perimeter to protect themselves from the incoming fire.

"6 Charlie, this is TOC. Ordered Cobra Gun Ships to your location," said the battalion commander.

"Roger that, smoke placed at our location, "said the Company C commander.

This initial burst inflicted casualties. The cries for "Medic" sounded, and the screams of hurt and anguish could be heard. Yet there was only one medic, leaving soldiers to seek the help of their friends to stop the bleeding, and apply first aid. Quickly, the company regrouped and maneuvered to counter the ambush. This failed and more casualties were sustained. The patrols returned back to their perimeter.

More calls for the medic to assist the wounded ensued. Usually, there was one medic for the company. Platoons often were in battle without a medic with them. At this contact, one medic went from one to another. He quickly moved under fire to assist the wounded, stabilizing them, and stopping the bleeding. RPG rounds flew overhead. Automatic, B-40 rockets, and small arms fire still penetrated the perimeter. But the rescue effort went on. Platoons assisted them, with members of their unit helping to pick up the wounded and transporting them either by litter or by carrying them with their arms.

Intense fire from the enemy continued as the unit withdrew to a landing zone. The company managed to backtrack on the trail despite the enemy fire and transported the wounded and dead soldier back to an LZ (Landing Zone).

A Medevac helicopter landed at the landing zone. The men quickly loaded up the wounded soldiers under fire. The LZ was "Hot!" Fortunately, the helicopter was able to leave with minor damage.

Company C formed a perimeter near the Landing Zone. The enemy directed accurate mortar and RPG (rifle propelled grenades) into the hard-pressed company. More casualties were incurred. The battalion commander sent Company A to aid Company C. Company A left firebase 25 to establish a corridor from the firebase to the location of Company C to help cover their withdrawal. The hostile fire became less, and the Company C commander was alerted to the fact that the enemy was moving to the rear of their location to counter Company A's movement toward them. He warned Company A's company commander.

"Alpha 6, this is Charlie 6. Movement headed toward you, lay down covering fire. NVA moving toward your location," said Charlie company commander.

"Charlie 6, this is Alpha 6. Roger that. Setting up Delta (defensive perimeter) now, "said the company commander of Company A. Company A continued to maintain their perimeter, as they still were getting sporadic fire into them. By staying in their defensive perimeter, they could withstand the volley. Finally, the enemy withdrew to the northwest, and the incoming fire ceased.

At this time Company C was now able to gather as many of the wounded and dead as possible to move from the battle site to the location of Company A. This combined forces and strengthened the defensive perimeter. Both companies were ordered back to fire support base 25 to regroup. This movement occurred without incident.

The battalion chaplain arrived at the fire support base 25 to meet with Company C to help grieve over the loss of their soldier. He arrived in the supply chopper. Chaplains are assigned to each Brigade and are non-denominational. This Chaplain was Baptist, but the chaplains were rotated, and different religious backgrounds could also arrive. The Chaplains were assigned and had an officer's rank. This Chaplain was the rank of Major. He gave a prayer for the dead soldier and comforted the troops. While he was doing that, the supplies were unloaded. The Chaplain finished his prayers, and quickly boarded the supply helicopter to return back to Brigade headquarters.

Casualties that Company C incurred included one killed in action (1 KIA) five missing in action (MIA) and twenty-eight wounded in action (WIA). Airstrikes dropped High Explosive (Phosphorous bombs) and napalm on the contact site area. Helicopter gunships (Cobra helicopters) were also called to direct machine gun and rocket fire on the area surrounding fire base 25 and on Nob Hill. Artillery also placed rounds throughout the night. But with all that, there was evidence the NVA still remained.

Intelligence reports surmised that the NVA were in well-fortified and strongly defended positions. Airstrikes and artillery were not as effective as desired. They built strongly constructed bunkers that could withstand airstrikes and artillery barrages in relative safety. Tunnels connected the bunkers. Concrete and steel were used along with natural stone and sod to make it withstand large bomb impacts and artillery. The size of the enemy force also increased to be regiment-sized or about 400 NVA. Because of their strategic positions any movement a friendly force outside of fire base 25 could be detected early. The NVA was also well supplied with ammunition, food, and supplies.

From the intelligence reports, the Battalion Commander decided after consultation with the company commanders that a tactical change is needed. The new strategy and tactic were to draw out the hostile forces into the open by initiating a feint attack. Once the elements were out in the open, the battalion would engage extensive mortar and artillery barrages. This would place a more effective fire on the enemy positions and do more damage to them. Prior to the start of this feint attack, TAC Air (Air Force F4 jet) was called for early morning bombing on NVA locations. This change in tactics offered our troops a way to overpower them.

The execution of the plan began on January 21, 1968. The first airstrike occurred at 0730 hours. Four additional strikes occurred every fifteen minutes. On each pass the fighter jets received automatic weapons fire. At 0945 hours artillery and mortar preparation fire penetrated the suspected locations. Fifteen minutes later (1000 hours) Company A departed fire base 25 to move toward the enemy locations and conduct the feint attack. (The battalion commander had all the leaders synchronize their watches.). Another barrage occurred fifteen minutes later at 1015 hours. The results of the barrage could not be determined due to the heavy jungle growth, but it was a covering fire to mask the oncoming feint attackers from Company A. Heavy fire from the hidden NVA positions (Machine gun, RPG, B-40 Rockets, and small arms fire AK-47) occurred, forcing it to form a defensive perimeter. The battalion commander did not want it to engage the NVA at this time as that would ruin the plans for a feint attack. Company A was immediately ordered to return to the fire support base and conduct the feint attack at a later time. However, a mission change occurred to redeploy the companies to other areas. It was believed that extensive damage was given to the NVA regiment, and that another attempt at a feint attack would not be a good strategy.

## Pork Chop Hill

That afternoon on January 21st Company B was airlifted to Dak To. Company D was deployed to defend the Ben Het Special Forces Camp, which had recently received incoming rounds from an unknown size force. While Company B was entering Ben Het encampment, its perimeter received 21 mortar rounds as well as RPG fire (Rifle propelled grenades). The combined forces fought back and fired artillery rounds at the hostile force area. There were no casualties, but two NVA bodies were spotted by a patrol the next morning. Company A and C, and the Reconnaissance platoon remained at firebase 25, as well as the artillery unit (105 howitzers) and the 4.2 mm Mortar team.

The mission at Fire Support Base 25 also changed. From field reports and observations, a large NVA unit believed to be another regiment-sized force (about 400 NVA) was located in the vicinity of Hill 800, now referred to as Pork Chop Hill. It was located about five kilometers northeast of Nob Hill, where the last combat activity took place.

The next day, patrols were continued from firebase 25 toward Nob Hill to locate the bodies of five men from Company C, and to determine the proximity of the enemy. Two bodies were recovered, and no contact was made. That find increased the number of soldiers killed in action (KIA) from Company C to 3, with 3 still missing (MIA). The search was continued in order to look for the three missing soldiers. Airstrikes continued periodically throughout the day on Nob Hill and its vicinity. The vicinity included Pork Chop Hill. There was no hostile fire coming from Nob Hill, but each time an aircraft passed over Pork Chop Hill, automatic weapons fire followed along with 50 caliber anti-aircraft rounds. The NVA moved from Nob Hill to Pork Chop Hill. Pork Chop Hill was the next objective.

On January 25th in the early morning hours, airstrikes were resumed with their sights on Pork Chop Hill and its vicinity. After an hour, the airstrikes ended. Mortars and artillery located at fire support base 25 began directing their fire on Pork Chop Hill. The battalion commander ordered Company A and C to depart the fire support base 25 to search for NVA around Pork Chop Hill. At 1230 hours Company A began receiving sniper fire. A platoon-sized force (about 40 men) opened fire from ambush positions with small arms, automatic weapons, B-40 rockets, and RPG (Rifle propelled grenades) from the front and flanks, causing light casualties. As the company (about 100 men) continued its valiant effort to continue its forward progress to seize Pork Hill, the enemy intensified its attack. Company A regrouped and sent the 1st platoon (20 men) to begin an assault on Pork Chop Hill. The remaining platoons placed covering fire for the platoon to advance and assume blocking positions. The first platoon assaulted on-line and moved up the hill toward the machine gun emplacement and the fortified bunkers. Each of the squads provided covering fire for the attacking squad and changed out to move up the hill slowly and methodically. Within 25 meters of the objective, the platoon threw grenades and directed machine gun fire into the bunker. The squads continued to interchange movement forward, firing extensively into the bunker area. Flame throwers were used when the platoon advanced within ten meters of the bunker. The platoon was successful in removing the threat and destroying a machine gun.

*Figure 16 82 MM Mortar Unit*

However, mortars (82 mm) that were concealed in the bunker complex and unable to be detected by aircraft still pounded Company A's perimeter, causing additional casualties. These mortars were still on Pork Chop Hill, despite losing one of their machine placements. The first platoon was ordered to return back to the perimeter of Company A. The platoon leader gave the order to withdraw.

"Alpha 1 this is Alpha 6, over," said the Company commander of Company A.

"6 this is 1. Machine gun silenced. Returning to Lima Quebec (Original patrol base location)," said the first platoon leader. The squads again moved one at a time, with the one placing covering fire on Pork Chop Hill, and the other moving forward. Then the opposite occurred. The platoon made it to the bottom without further casualties and began moving to the company's location. The withdrawal was successful.

The first platoon started on their return back to the company patrol base. Sporadic sniper fire hindered their movement. "Spider Holes" also were encountered along the trail. ("Spider Holes" were holes with ridiculously small openings that were about five foot deep. The occupants of the hole were totally concealed with vegetation covering the hole. It was a perfect place to hide and ambush troops as they moved down the trail.) The platoon leader decided to move off the trail and cut a new trail to go back to the base. This took much longer than expected. But by doing this they did not encounter any more hostile fire and were able to continue to progress toward the company patrol base without any further incidents.

Company C, which had moved with the progress of Company A was taking casualties from mortars and snipers. Company C's movement was parallel to Company A. The Battalion Commander ordered both companies to return back to the fire support base 25. The battalion commander believed that there was a security threat to the base. As soon as the companies entered the base, the NVA unit promptly re-directed its mortars. Incoming rounds into the fire support base were intense. Their target was the 4.2 mortars and artillery guns which provided support for the operation. The rounds managed to enter the bunker area where the mortars were located. This caused three of the men shooting the mortar rounds to be injured. Another enemy round landed within the parapet (storage area for ammunition) where the 4.2 rounds are stored. This caused a large explosion as the area around the parapet was ignited and in them the mortars. The resulting fire spread across the northern portion of the perimeter toward the main ammunition and mortar storage area. The soldiers rallied to put out the fires and distinguished themselves by selflessly braving flying shrapnel and mortars to extinguish the blaze. At 2230 hours the fire was under control. As a result, 2000 rounds of mortars which were stored in the main storage area were spared and saved. The fire was put out with limited resources, as water was sparse. The men started a bucket brigade from a mountain stream, 100 meters from the fire support base. The buckets traveled up and down the chain. Finally, the fire was put out. Other members of the company smothered the blaze with their ponchos and jungle blankets, as well as placing dirt on the flames.

Patrols were sent out from the fire support base and were able to capture five enemy soldiers. They were interrogated at length and then moved on to the rear areas for further questioning.

The day ended with a high casualty count. There were seven soldiers killed in action (KIA) and twenty-seven soldiers wounded (WIA). The enemy casualties were unable to be determined, outside of five NVA bodies spotted near the contact site. Information received from NVA prisoners captured from the conflict indicated that many more were killed and wounded from the intense fire fight. Reconnaissance missions reaffirmed that account, as blood trails were found and drag marks where the wounded were taken away.

# The "Peanut"

The following two days were dedicated to evaluating the intelligence reports and the lessons learned reports. It was determined that at least one NVA regiment (about 400 men) was operating around fire support base 25 and another regiment surrounded Ben Het Special Forces Camp. Reports also indicated that another NVA company (about 100 men) was in the area, but their location was not known.

Because of the dense undergrowth and triple canopy jungle there was only one tactical route available to conduct an attack on the regiments that were harassing Fire Support Base 25, Fire Support Base 13, Bridge 3, Ben Het Special Forces Camp, Dak to Village, and the remnants of forces surrounding Pork Chop Hill. The brigade commander and staff believed that the ARVN Battalion (Army of the "Republic of Vietnam) 6th Airborne Division and the 3rd Battalion, 12th Infantry, 4th Infantry Division should conduct a joint and coordinated operation against the NVA units in the area. The short-range objective was to eliminate the pressures exerted against firebase 25 while the overall plan was to eliminate all NVA combat soldiers in the area that were threatening Ben Het and Dak To. The size of all NVA units in this area was estimated to be about 1000 strong combat troops. Usually there is about a 3 to 1 ratio of support troops to a combat troop, or the total estimated force may be as much as 4000 men. These were the best estimates derived from intelligence reports.

The ARVN airborne unit would conduct a helicopter assault upon Dog Hill and would continue to seize Bear Ridge. Both of these Hills were about four kilometers north and about

7 kilometer east of Pork Chop Hill. Once the unit secured both these objectives, it would continue to move toward the south and join the 3rd Battalion, 12th Infantry to seize the "Peanut." The Peanut was located about 3 kilometers north of the Ben Het Special Forces Camp. This operation was designed to force the enemy to fight on different fronts and weakening their strength in this area.

In preparation for this operation, the battalion needed to redistribute its elements. Company D, which was located at Ben Het Special Forces Camp, was airlifted to fire support base 25. Company B which had been at Dak To moved its second platoon to join the battalion's reconnaissance platoon at Bridge 3, about 3 kilometers northeast of Fire Support Base 25. The remainder of Company B went to firebase 13, which is located about 4 kilometers east of Ben Het Special Forces Camp.

On the morning of January 26th artillery and mortar fire were directed at Pork Chop Hill, the "Peanut", Dog Hill, and Bear Ridge to prepare for an oncoming assault. At 0829 hours the 6th Airborne ARVN troops landed by helicopter on Dog Hill without incident. Simultaneously, Company C and D 3rd Bn. 12th Infantry departed fire support base 25 with Company D the lead unit. It began receiving incoming fire when they were about 200 meters from Pork Chop Hill. The company commander of Company D directed two platoons to conduct an on-line assault up the sides of the hill to gain fire superiority. Each squad of both platoons used the tactic of one squad moving to the top, and the other covering them. The platoons continued to receive intense RPG fire, small arms, and automatic weapons as they slowly went up the hill. Company C, which had been following Company D from fire support base 25, had two platoons maneuver forward to be at the flanks of Company D's two platoons as they advanced up the hill. Sniper fire harassed both companies as they conducted maneuvers. The NVA strategically placed "Spider Holes" along the hillside. The sole purpose of the "spider hole" was to slow down the attacking elements so that the remainder of the NVA could withdraw safely and avoid capture.

While Company C was backing up Company D's movement up the hill, patrols began a search for the "spider holes" and tree snipers in order to challenge the snipers and eliminate their threat to Company D that existed along the flanks. The patrols were spread out from the trails to carefully observe the area. When a "spider hole" was spotted, the squads split up into elements and approached the "spider holes" from both sides to eliminate the threat. The tree snipers posed a different problem, since their vision was far greater than the ones in the "spider holes." To counteract this threat, five soldiers climbed trees to counteract the tree snipers. This proved successful but slow, as the tree climbers had to climb several trees to spot a sniper. As a result of this effort, over 30 "spider holes" were found and destroyed, and about ten tree snipers were eliminated.

Once the snipers were eliminated, Company D reached the top of Pork Chop Hill by eliminating a machine gun bunker with grenades, flame throwers, and small arms fire. When the top was reached Company D started a systematic and steady assault from bunker to bunker. The method used was the following. First the grenade launchers placed fire into the bunker. Flame throwers moved to within ten meters of the bunker, and small arms fire continued to fire into the bunker. At times, the NVA soldiers emerged from the bunker and attacked. In many instances the fighting was hand to hand combat. The fighting was extremely intense in close combat. The soldiers used their machetes and pistols to fight. The US soldiers proved stronger than their NVA counterparts and captured and killed them. NVA Machine guns and RPG continued to fire into members of Company D. Finally, after four hours of maneuvering up Pork Chop Hill, and fighting for one hour of hand to hand combat, the NVA were killed and/or captured or escaped. Mortar fire was directed on the troops as they fought gallantly on the top.

By 1335 hours the enemy was driven from Pork Chop Hill. The enemy soldiers were observed going northeast leaving the area. Harassing fire hindered efforts of Company D to follow the enemy out of the hill. The Company Commander called the platoons back to search the area. The units began searching the hill for weapons and bodies of the missing soldiers. They found all of the American bodies (3) missing from the contact on January 20$^{th}$. Also found were the bodies of seventeen NVA soldiers. During the conflict, Company D lost four soldiers killed in action (KIA) and eleven soldiers wounded in action (WIA).

Meanwhile the South Vietnamese Army (ARVN) encountered multiple enemy forces. The ARVN airborne unit began encountering extremely heavy enemy resistance in its drive to the south. It was reported that both sides were taking moderate to heavy casualties. Because of the extremely slow progress of the ARVN forces, the assault on the “Peanut” was delayed for twenty-four hours.

On January 25th Companies A , 3rd Battalion 12th Infantry and Company C, 1st BN, 8th Infantry were airlifted to Bear Ridge and assumed security of that hill. Company C, 3rd Battalion, 12th Infantry commenced an attack on the “Peanut”. As three platoons were placed online to assault, intense enemy small arms, automatic weapons, RPG (rifle propelled grenades), and B-40 rockets directed fire on the moving line. Company C regrouped and had one platoon continue the assault with the other two platoons protecting the flanks and deploying their fire from side to side. The three platoons moved forward slowly. It took the platoons three days to be within reach of the top of the hill. On the fourth day, one of the platoons finally made it to the same level as the entrenched NVA. As soon as the platoon appeared at the top of the hill, the NVA quickly withdrew from their bunkers and moved from the top of hill in the opposite direction. The platoons quickly secured the top of the "Peanut." Once it was secured, the wounded were evacuated by helicopter. There were no fatalities in this encounter with the NVA in this intense battle. The "Peanut" was searched after the contact. Three graves were found that contained the bodies of the men assigned to Company B who had been missing since January 19th. Also found was a diary and other military documents that indicated the enemy was part of the 66th NVA regiment. This regiment was an elite and highly trained NVA force. It was further believed that the force which defended the hill was a delaying force for the withdrawal of a larger unit. The action of the "Peanut" lasted until January 28th, or into the 4th day of intense fighting. Peanut

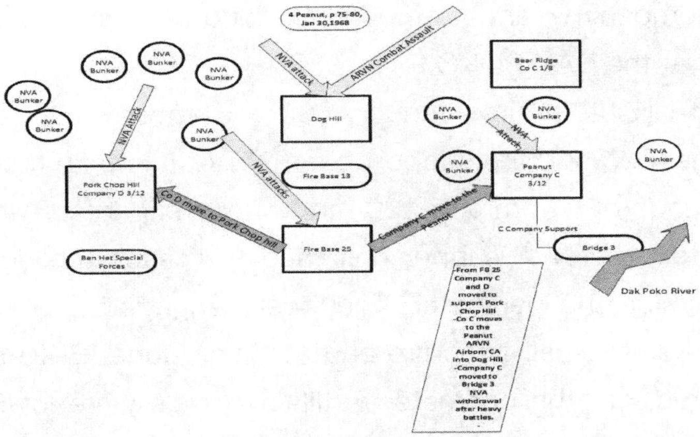


*Schematic Drawing 4— Peanut*

# DAK POKO RIVER AND BRIDGE 3 JAN 30TH-FEB 4TH

Activity was light for January 29th and 30th due to the proposed TET truce. Company C and D moved back to fire support base 25 without incident. (TET was a New Year's celebration recognized by all of Vietnam.) Intelligence information that was compiled indicated that the enemy intended to launch a massive ground attack against Dak to and the ARVN military installation at Tanh Canh within the next few days. Another prime target was thought to be Bridge 3, since its destruction would cut off Ben Het Special Forces Camp. Also, it would cut off point's south on Highway 512. It was determined that the enemy would cross the DAK POKO River which ran east of firebase 25.

Company A and Company D departed firebase 25 and arrived at the DAK POKO River.

At 1742 hours January 30th Company C reported movement around fire support base 25. At this time more than 150 rounds of 82mm and 120 mm rounds impacted within the perimeter. The NVA sapper unit tried to breach the defensive wire outside the perimeter. They were engaged by Company C with heavy small arms fire and machine guns. B-40 rockets were fired into the perimeter. Artillery barrels were lowered to direct the fire at point blank range. This stopped the enemy from breaching the perimeter. The next morning, the outside perimeter area was searched by a platoon sweep. The soldiers found four NVA bodies, and 1 SKS rifle, 1 RPG, 1 Magazine, 2 pole charges, and 3 AK47 rifles (Made in China). The equipment found indicated that sappers had been prepared to attempt to enter the perimeter while the remainder of the enemy stood by in the hopes of launching a ground attack.

For the next eleven days, action remained light with only sporadic incoming mortars hitting firebase 25. In addition, Bridge 3, manned by the second platoon of Company B and the reconnaissance platoon withstood two abortive weapons attacks and two sapper attacks. On February 9th, a patrol from Company D captured an NVA officer in the vicinity near the Dak Poko River. Through interrogation the officer admitted he was a senior Captain and the Division surgeon for the 1st NVA division. He stated that between the periods of January 26th to 29th that he had personally treated over 400 NVA soldiers that were wounded in action as a result of the action near fire support base 25. He also told of the more than 200 NVA soldiers that were killed during the same period. Another NVA prisoner that was captured on February $10^{th}$ revealed that elements of the $66^{th}$ NVA Regiment had established a base camp and hospital complex in Ngoh Ting Tong or Hill 886.

On February $12^{th}$ fire support base 25 was subjected to a weapons attack as two squads were changing reliefs at a listening/observation post. The two squads were subjected to heavy small arms fire and automatic weapons. A platoon was deployed to assist. The enemy continued to fire on the squads and the platoon members that were sent to assist them. Another platoon was sent to the contact site. This platoon included a 50-caliber machine gun and four flame throwers to reinforce the units under fire. By 1308 hours the enemy was destroyed, with the remainder withdrawing from the area.

A search of the contact site revealed that the enemy had built hastily constructed fighting positions from fallen logs and each position was linked together with a trench. Also, the trench system extended parallel to the perimeter for 150 meters. There were quickly dug bunkers with communication lines. Many weapons and equipment were found, including a Chicom heavy machine gun with wheel carriage for transporting.

The threat to Dak To had been diminished substantially. The enemy had been defeated in a number of engagements, throughout the $3^{rd}$ Battalion, $12^{th}$ Infantry area of operations. The enemy had been defeated in a number of engagements. Company A and D swept the area surrounding Ngok Ting Tong and had no contacts or incidents. The $6^{th}$ ARVN airborne withdrew to the south. Artillery, air strikes, and massive B-52 Bomber strikes weakened the enemy.

# Command Hill

It was believed that the enemy would try to desperately save face by launching an attack against either the Ben Het Special Forces Camp or fire support base 13 where Company C and the reconnaissance platoon were located. Further intelligence indicated that the 66$^{th}$ NVA regiment had a base camp in the vicinity. Company A and B prepared to be airlifted into Command Hill (referred by the military as Hill 651) to locate and destroy the 66$^{th}$ NVA regiment.

Both companies were airlifted to a landing zone, located near Serenity Hill on February 26$^{th}$. The first helicopter to reach the landing zone carried five troops and landed without incident. The troops immediately began securing the landing zone. The second helicopter encountered heavy fire. The landing zone was hot! The helicopter could not hover over the landing zone and attempted to leave. However, the enemy fire caused it to crash. This obstructed the landing zone and prevented the other helicopters from arriving. The four crewman and the five troops in the helicopter joined the first troops on the ground to begin to return fire on the NVA bunkers. The crew members crawled from the downed chopper to go to the other five that were returning fire. Automatic weapon fire was fired over their heads. Finally, they were able to join the other team members. The Battalion Commander as he was hovering over the landing zone relayed that there were 25 fortified bunker positions. Cobra gunships were requested to fire on the NVA.

"TOC, this is 1 Bravo. Five pinned down on the ground, receiving fire. 2$^{nd}$ chopper crew arrived at our LZ. We are receiving fire from the northwest. Can you assist? Over," said the 1st platoon leader of Company B.

"1 Bravo, this is TOC. Observed 25 enemy bunkers surrounding LZ. Calling in artillery and gunship support for you. Moving choppers to another LZ. Over," said the Battalion Commander.

*Figure 17 105 Howitzer*

"Roger that, fire for effect. Smoke on the ground, "said the 1st platoon leader from Company B.

The gunships began arriving to cover the positions while an alternative landing zone was determined.

The other troops were to land at an alternate Landing Zone. It was located about 200 meters northwest of the original landing zone area. The first helicopter landed without incident. This one included the company commander of Company B. The next helicopter though encountered small arms fire, which wounded the pilot. The co-pilot took control of the craft and moved it from the landing zone. The landing zone was now Hot! The company commander along with the four troops was surrounded by the enemy. The situation in both landing zones was grave.

"TOC, this is 6 Bravo. Huey landed. The second could not. Moved to another LZ. We are surrounded and receiving heavy fire. Pinned down. Returning fire. Need support. Over," said the Company Commander of B.

"Roger that, 6 Bravo. 1Bravo 200 meters from you pinned down. Stay down and return fire. Gunships will cover you, "said the Battalion Commander.

"1 Bravo, this is TOC. Disengage the enemy and move 200 meters to meet up with 6 Bravo. Over," said the Battalion Commander.

"Roger that. Will move ASAP. Still receiving fire," said the 1st platoon leader.

"6 Bravo, this is 1 Bravo. Moving toward you. Over," said the 1st platoon leader.

"Roger that 1 Bravo. Receiving fire also. Move out. Over," said the B Company Commander.

"Am OK. Moving Out!" said the 1st platoon leader.

The element moved away from the first LZ to join Company B Commander. They moved under fire to join them. The small element of thirteen formed a small perimeter to protect them and to fire on the enemy positions. Artillery strikes were directed from there. The remainder of Company B that landed on the alternate landing zone, made their way toward the thirteen still under fire. The 2nd platoon leader led it. They were able to join the small element and set up a perimeter.

The following day on February 27th Company B and the reconnaissance platoon were preparing to attack the hill. The company began receiving 82 mm mortar rounds that impacted into its perimeter, causing some light casualties. Artillery fire was directed to the area where the mortars were located. Within seconds after the artillery rounds pounded the suspected hostile force locations, NVA were observed along the wood line. Company B quickly redeployed to their defensive positions on the opposite side of the perimeter. At 0839 hours it was completely surrounded by hundreds of attacking NVA soldiers. The fire received by the company was extremely intense. Finally, after gallantly fighting the onslaught, the assault was repulsed after it reached within 15 meters of the perimeter. The NVA quickly dispersed and withdrew. There were many NVA casualties from this contact. Artillery and mortar fire barrages continued around the perimeter.

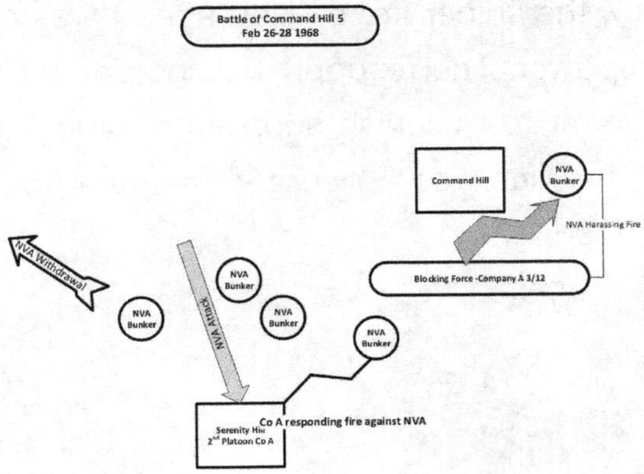


*Schematic Drawing 5—Command Hill*

Once withdrawn from battle, the NVA continued intense small arms fire, automatic weapons, RPG and B-40 rockets from their hilltop emplacements and placed the fire into the perimeter. They again attacked and moved forward. Airstrikes were called to drop ordinance on the perimeter to stop the attacking enemy. Napalm was dropped about 15 meters outside the defensive bunkers. At 1041 hours a lull occurred in the fighting. Artillery was again directed and adjusted to follow the NVA retreating route. At 1143 hours the NVA regrouped and again attacked with intensity. Both artillery and airstrikes were called, to direct their fire on the believed locations. The incoming fire ceased as the NVA again withdrew and regrouped. The attack ended at 1251 hours.

The company's ammunition supply was critically low. It was in fact at the critical stage. Snipers continued to harass the perimeter and fired at will on incoming resupply helicopters and Medevac helicopters which prevented them from landing. Continuous artillery fire and airstrikes focused on sightings of the sniper fire. Finally, the sniper fire ceased after it was overcome by the heavy firepower. The resupply helicopters were able to land without incident to replenish supplies of ammunition and other supplies. The Medevac helicopter was able to land and remove the wounded.

*Figure 18 MedEvac Helicopter*

Later that evening, more movement was detected. Airstrikes were called to drop high explosives (HE) and napalm on their positions. At 0055 hours a small NVA unit on February 28th maneuvered within 15 meters of the perimeter. They fired B40 rockets and RPG into it causing light casualties. The units returned fire and repelled them.

Meanwhile, Company A, which was placed in a blocking position on the other side of Command Hill, engaged the NVA by moving up the hill on an on-line assault. They encountered heavy fire as well and withdrew back to their perimeter to return fire. The Company A Commander directed artillery strikes on the fortified bunkers. At mid-day, the NVA army seemed to disappear and contact with them ended. Company A maintained their defensive perimeter, receiving sniper fire and harassing small arms fire. Their perimeter continued to be probed. During the night movement was detected, but no new action occurred.

When daylight came, many NVA bodies and equipment were found in front of the perimeter. There were drag marks also, indicating that some of the enemy was dragged from the battle site. The NVA was believed to have suffered a severe blow. They had been virtually destroyed. However, the US lost five killed in action. The NVA dead were 111.

During the period January 11 to February 28th, 1968, the 3rd Battalion 12th Infantry engaged units of the NVA in ground combat on nine separate occasions. Seven of contacts surrounded fire support base 25 when patrols encountered small units of NVA in the area. Fire support base 13 had two incidents of contacts as well.

From the January and February campaigns, the 3rd Battalion, 12th Infantry lost twenty-seven men killed in action.

NVA losses were 184 killed in action. Intelligence reported that the result of the questioning of the NVA surgeon captured in battle at Pork Chop Hill revealed that the 66th NVA regiment had suffered more than 600 casualties as a result of the actions near fire support base 25 during the period of January 26th to 29th. Of these the NVA lost more than 200 that were killed. A commander for the 8th Battalion, 66th NVA regiment who was also captured at Pork Chop Hill after this period stated that the 7th Battalion, 66th regiment had been virtually destroyed and a second battalion badly mauled. With both men stating that the strength of the NVA regiment operating near Pork Chop Hill was lessened considerably and most likely rebuilding, the 3rd Bn. 12th Infantry battalion was returned to Camp Enari to regroup, receive new troops, and conduct patrols around the base.

Patrols from February on in 1968 were concentrated on areas around Camp Enari and Highways 14 and 19. The battalion supported "Thunder Road" which was a convoy of tanks and infantry working together on patrols along the highways.

*Figure 19 Tank used for "Thunder Road" Road Clearing Operation*

At night, the troops were stationed at Camp Enari in barracks. They also were on defensive duty at night to man the many bunkers, as well as assist artillery in moving ammunition from the parapets. Contacts were light in that period although they would occur without warning or intelligence

Movement was detected by a listening post near a bridge about 15 kilometers west of Camp Enari along Highway 19. It started out to be just another night of guard duty. With the warning from the listening post a platoon was alerted to observe intently in the moon light to be alert for any suspicious activity. One of them noticed something or someone in the water, and quickly alerted the platoon members. The object was a raft.

The platoon leader gave the order to fire on the raft with M16 rifles and M60 machine gun against it. A flare was immediately lit and projected above. The raft was loaded with 400 lbs. of explosive ordnance.

The raft, even though receiving incoming fire from the platoon, kept on course toward the bridge. It was unmanned, and the incoming fire failed to sink the raft. It finally rested on the pilings underneath the bridge. The raft was about eight feet long, five feet wide, and constructed of thick bamboo poles. However, the platoon received a shock of their life. It was loaded with a 250 lb. aerial bomb, a RPG, B-40 rockets, C-4 explosives and fuse wire, and another 150 lb. home-made bomb. The Viet Cong had planned to blow up the bridge and then use that to attack the bridge security force. It was believed that the VC were actually manning the raft and guiding it toward the bridge. But when the firing started, they left the boat unmanned. The quick thinking by our platoon in disrupting its path by firing into it saved lives and contacts with the VC.

Now the real trick began as the bombs had to be destroyed. The raft was moved down river to a safer location. Engineers were called in to explode the cargo. Dynamite was placed throughout the raft, and the engineers departed quickly. “Fire in the Hole” was shouted to warn of the impending explosion. All were told to take cover. The raft was destroyed, along with the other ordnance.

The raft was blown up and the shrapnel from the bombs scattered for over 400 yards from the explosion. The men finally relaxed after this, thanking the listening post for alerting them about this incident. The VC is very elusive, and this would have been an extremely hard hit and run by them. Fortunately, no damage was done this time.

# CHAPTER FOUR COMBAT OPERATIONS 1969

## *Plei Trap Valley*

From agent observations and other intelligence reports, the $24^{th}$ NVA (North Vietnamese Army) regiment and the sapper unit began staging to prepare for an attack on Kontum, the Polei Kleng Special Forces camp, and the fire support bases west of Polei Kleng. Because of this information, and because of the waning Viet Cong activity surrounding the Camp Enari area and Pleiku City in January and early February 1969, the $3^{rd}$ Battalion, $12^{th}$ Infantry and their direct support artillery battery B Battery $6^{th}$ Battalion $29^{th}$ Artillery, were ordered to commence operation Wayne Grey near Plei Mrong and Polei Kheng Special Forces camp.

*Figure 20 Heliborne Assault Early Morning Movement*

A helicopter combat assault was planned to enter an abandoned fire base named LZ Swinger located West of Polei Kleng which was in the Plei Trap Valley, Kontum Province. The mission was to search for NVA units, confront them, and halt their progress. Also attached to the battalion was an engineering unit, which constructed roads heavy enough to transport heavy artillery, large convoys, and trains. It would construct buildings to house mess (meals), medical outpost, sleeping quarters, headquarter buildings, and an air strip. It also constructed parapets to store ammunition, bombs, and supplies. Parapets are concealed fortified storage areas. Fortified bunkers were constructed around the perimeter, along with barbed wire to protect the Landing Zone from hostile forces. A minefield was also constructed in designated locations around the perimeter.

Additional intelligence reports were provided to the command and staff. The reports identified two well-equipped NVA infantry units, the 24$^{th}$ regiment and the 66$^{th}$ NVA regiments, operating around Polei Kleng It was estimated to be the strength of about 2800 combat troops and about twice that number of support troops or 5600 support personnel. Moreover, the Plei Trap Valley area was considered to be a stronghold for the NVA and was supported by roads into Cambodia and Laos where the units could transport artillery and supplies. Heavy trucks were used to bring equipment, mostly during the night, to NVA units. The Ho Chi Minh Trail passed through the valley, one of the main infiltration routes used by North Vietnam to enter South Vietnam.

On March 1, 1969, Company A conducted a combat assault from Plei Mrong airstrip at 0700 hours into an abandoned fire support base LZ Swinger. Intense artillery preparation and an air strike preceded the initial element's landing. Yet, in spite of these precautionary measures, a reinforced company- sized force (about 100 NVA soldiers), hidden in fortified bunkers, initiated contact. For three hours, helicopters threaded their way through intense fire to land the remainder of Company A. Close artillery support and napalm strikes were placed on the landing zone perimeter but could not affect the concentration of the incoming rounds. Landings were made under fire. The LZ was Hot! To further add to the struggle of landing, the troops on the ground uncovered anti-personnel and anti-helicopter mines that were scattered by the NVA throughout the LZ, hampering resupply efforts and the additional landing of troop. Furthermore, assault tactics could not be used to counterattack against the entrenched enemy off of the landing zone area due to the machine gun fire, RPG, and small arms fire that constantly sprayed into the perimeter of the LZ. Finally, after five hours being hit by a barrage of artillery rounds and over 100 bombs, it forced the NVA Company to withdraw to the North. The landing zone was secured by 1310 hours; six hours after the initial helicopter assault began.

Company A then reconsolidated their unit, secured LZ Swinger, and waited on the arrival of an artillery unit, C battery 92$^{nd}$ artillery. Defensive positions were secured with sandbags, and fire position holes were dug to weather incoming rounds. Parapets were established to store the ammunition. A battalion train's area to receive supplies was established. The area was also swept with a mine detector to ensure that the hidden mines of the landing zone area were not in this perimeter. Patrols were established to sweep the immediate area. Listening posts (LP) were placed in strategic locations, especially along trails. Movement throughout the evening and night were detected by the Listening Posts (LP's).

"6 Alpha, this is Lima Papa 2," said the listening post on the south trail location.

"Go ahead, over," said the A Company Commander.

"Movement on our right side. Spotted 3 NVA soldiers on the trail. Moving toward your location. Over," said the listening post.

"Are they on top of you?" asked the A Company Commander.

"Yes, over," said the listening post.

"Blow your claymore mines, and come back to the perimeter," said the A Company Commander.

The claymore mines were blown and the 2nd listening post entered the perimeter. The other two listening posts also heard movement and called artillery fire on those locations. Their positions were not compromised. Sniper fire into the perimeter continued throughout the night. The other two listening posts continued to monitor the situation. LP 2 returned back to their position once the enemy fire lessened in the evening. All three listening posts were in position after 2200 hours.

Patrols that searched the immediate area around the perimeter found 30 NVA soldiers left on the battlefield, and an unknown number that were wounded. The patrols noted that there were blood trails and drag marks. Company A incurred 1 KIA and 13 WIA during this engagement.

One NVA soldier was captured. The prisoner was interrogated. The result of the questioning was the following:

- Company A combat assaulted into a main resupply route junction.
- The American move was known three weeks in advance before the actual assault.

- Much preparation had been made by both regiments to prevent the establishment of the firebase.
- Final warning by the prisoner that the firebase would be subject to constant probes, heavy weapons attacks, and ground attacks.

The remaining companies (Company B, C, and D, and the engineer battalion) of the Battalion completed the convoy movement from Plei Mrong to the firebase LZ Mary Lou. This location was designated for the battalion trains during this operation. There were reports of no further enemy action that day.

The battalion marched from LZ Mary Lou at 0820 to the Polei Kleng Special Forces camp. From there, the reconnaissance platoon was transported to LZ Mary Lou by helicopter followed by 2nd platoon, Company D, and the heavy mortar platoon. At 1513 hours, Company C established a patrol base, about 2 kilometers North from LZ Swinger. Company B then was inserted to establish another patrol base, about 2 kilometers South from LZ Mary. Each insertion was not confronted by the enemy force.

All troop movement to the scheduled landing zones was completed and the artillery unit was in place—Battery B, 6th Battalion, 29th artillery with Company C at LZ Swinger. Company D was placed also at LZ Mary Lou. Company A remained at LZ Swinger. The battalion fire support base at LZ Swinger had 2 companies, an artillery battalion, and supports (Medical and Mess) as well as being the main resupply point. No further enemy contact occurred until March 4th.

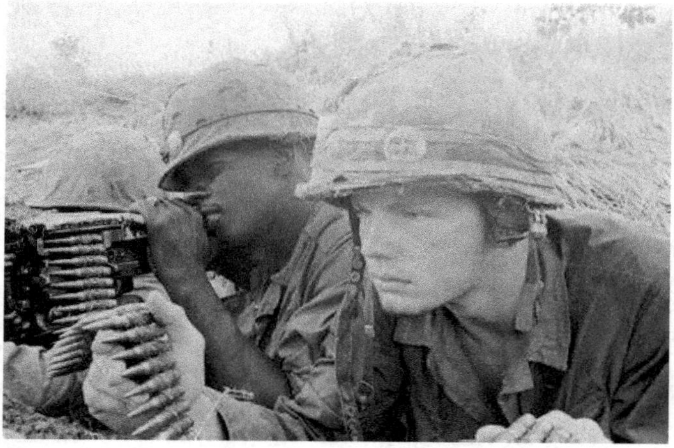

*Figure 21 Defensive positions*

On March 4, 1969, the prisoner's forecast became a reality. At 0325 hours not only did LZ Swinger receive a heavy bombardment of 105 howitzer fire in the early morning hours, but also simultaneously Polei Kleng air strip 122 mm rockets. Then later that morning at 1010 hours Polei Kleng airstrip was subjected to an enemy's weapons attack. Helicopters and planes on the airstrip received B-40 rocket fire as well as rifle propelled grenades (RPG). One helicopter was disabled. A call went to A troop, 7th Squadron, 17th Air Cavalry to conduct a helicopter assault on the firing positions that damaged the airport. Quickly the 1st Air Cavalry units went out at first light, located the positions, dropped the soldiers on the ground to attack and were able to extinguish the enemy fire. The weapons attacks ceased. A troop, 7th squadron, 17th Air Cavalry returned back to the Polei Kleng encampment. It was a typical quick hit by this outstanding unit. There were no friendly casualties, and NVA casualties were unknown.

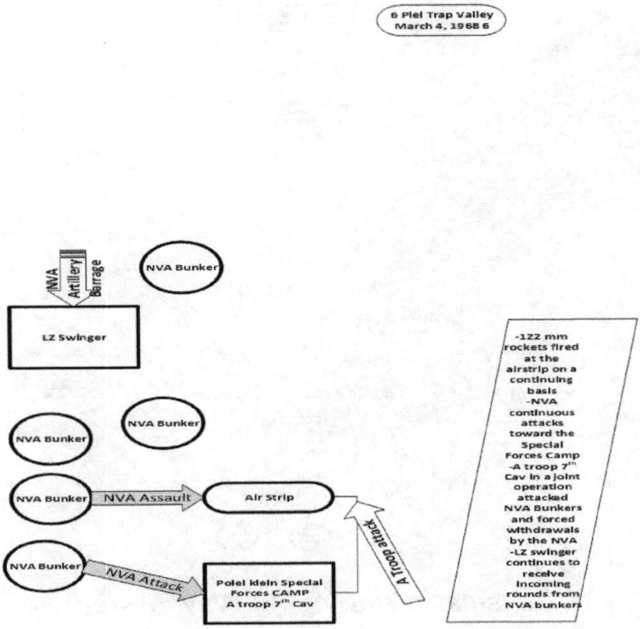


*Schematic Drawing 6-Plei Trap Valley*

On March 5, 1969, the 3d Battalion, 12th Infantry was ordered to establish blocking positions to trap withdrawing enemy forces. The 3rd Battalion 8th Infantry had encountered a large NVA unit. Immediately they received small arms fire, automatic weapons, and mortar rounds when the platoons engaged the enemy. Artillery and gunships were employed against them. The NVA withdrew and ceased fire. The 3rd Battalion, 12th Infantry was moved from LZ Swinger to establish a blocking force to contain the enemy and destroy them. The strategy worked, and the NVA unit withdrew from the contact and moved away from the blocking force. An extensive short range patrol network was established to search for remnants of the NVA units and engage them. Company C was airlifted back to LZ Swinger, and Company B was extracted back to LZ Mary Lou.

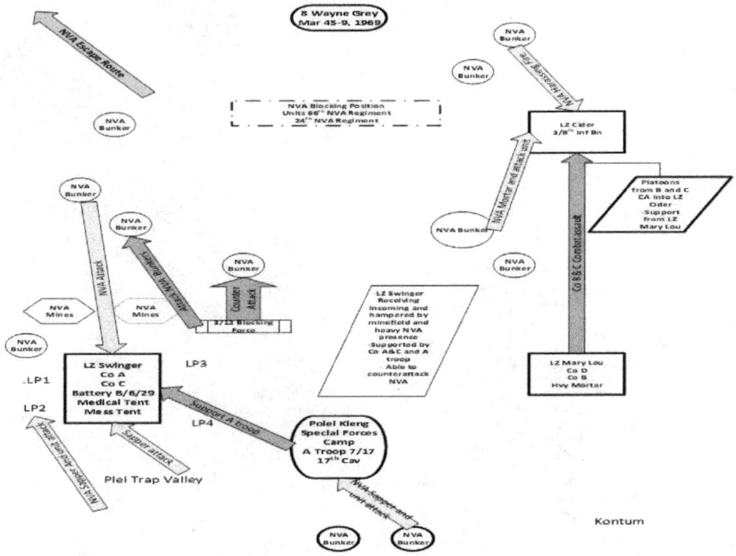


*Schematic Drawing 7—Wayne Grey*

# *Task Force Swift*

Faced with growing strength of the enemy forces, which was able to resupply themselves despite air observations and bombings, the brigade commander determined that a blocking force would not be sufficient to destroy enemy forces. He then ordered the formation of Task Force Swift. The Brigade commander ordered Company D and Company C to combat assault from LZ Swinger (C Company) and LZ Mary (B Company) into the area where 3rd Battalion, 8th Infantry was attacked by the large enemy forces and assist them in the security of their fire support base. Also, the two units were to replace and reinforce the depleted ranks of that unit. Task Force Swift swept an area south- southwest but did not have any significant contact. Company B formed a perimeter, awaiting the arrival of the other Task Force Company, Company C to arrive. Each platoon was given a sector to defend. Three listening posts were placed in location for the night. The 82 mm detachment put their weapons in place, readied for the next movement.

By 1855 hours only two sorties (helicopters) landed with soldiers from Company C. The remainder was to be transported at first light the next morning. Throughout that evening and into the next morning March 7, enemy movement was noted by the listening posts of Task Force Swift.

"6 Bravo, this is Lima Papa 2, saw shadows moving among the trees. There are definite signs of movement around the perimeter, over," said the 2nd listening post squad leader.

"Lima Papa 2, is 6 Bravo. Keep observing. If it comes too close, move back to the perimeter. Do not disclose your position. We are getting probed also," said the B Company Commander.

The main force of Company B was probed by rocks thrown by unknown sources to see if the guard posts were awake and alert. It looked as if the rock throwing was timed at every 20-minute intervals from 0030 hours to 0430 hours. The next day at 1000 hours, helicopters picked up Company B of Task Force Swift and airlifted into location without incident.

On March 8th, Company B of Task Force Swift moved forward to its objective at LZ Brace unopposed and continued its sweep south to link with Company D, 3rd Battalion, 8th Infantry, and Company C, 3rd Battalion, 12th Infantry. Air strikes and artillery were fired on suspected enemy locations. On numerous occasions when Company B stopped for the night, there were more movements and probes. The same thing was noted a 20-minute interval of rock throwing that focused on various parts of the patrol base. The listening post encountered one NVA soldier stealthily moving toward their location. The listening post fired volleys at him, and then moved back into the perimeter. That night, six sappers tried to breach the perimeter, but were repelled by quick action from the 1st platoon. Casualties sustained by the NVA during the period from March 1, 1969, to March 8th were 241 killed in action, and an unknown number of wounded. Friendly losses, most of which were sustained by Company D, 3rd Battalion, 8th Infantry were 32 killed in action (KIA), 125 wounded in action (WIA), and 1 missing in action (MIA).

Even though Task Force Swift secured the objective, it continued to operate out of a patrol base. At 0827 hours on March 9, a short-range reconnaissance patrol (SRP) from Company C contacted an NVA squad (about 8 men). It returned to the perimeter to inform the unit of the activity at LZ Swinger. It was again hit by 105 mm Howitzer Fire and 82 mm Mortar Fire. Airstrikes and Artillery countered the fire. 9 NVA soldiers were killed, and an unknown amount was wounded. Friendly losses included 4 US soldiers dead (KIA) and 14 wounded (WIA).

The next morning on March 10 the determined NVA unit struck LZ Swinger again with 105 mm Howitzer rounds and 82 mm mortar rounds. This caused 1 US killed in action (KIA) and 14 US wounded in action (WIA). It was countered by artillery, mortars, and airstrikes. The NVA stealthily camouflaged their departure back to their hidden bunkers to wait until the next day. No other action occurred in that afternoon and evening. Ammunition and supplies were transported into LZ Swinger by resupply helicopters without incident. The wounded were removed by Medevac as well as the dead soldier. The battalion chaplain also came with the resupply helicopter to give remembrance to the fallen soldier and comfort those that needed it. The chaplain then returned back on the resupply helicopter to the battalion trains area. Chaplains are considered non-denominational, but this one was a Roman Catholic priest who was serving his tour as the Battalion chaplain. It was a short visit, but a welcome one for those who face adversity and hostile fire.

Throughout that night Task Force Swifts listening posts detected enemy movement. At 0500 hours March 11 LZ Swinger was again under an NVA weapons attack by 105 Howitzers and 82mm Mortars. The fire was again countered by artillery and airstrikes. Then at 0900 hours Task Force Swift's patrol base received over 100 rounds of mortar fire. At 1145 hours Short Range Reconnaissance Patrol (SRP) of Company C found 4 NVA killed in action (KIA) and fresh blood trails. The second platoon of Company C was dispatched to reinforce the SRP and to direct an airstrike on the suspected NVA locations. Yet the question remains as to the whereabouts of the NVA unit since the triple canopy jungle seems to conceal exact locations. The airstrike was directed to hit in the general vicinity of the sounds of the mortar weapons, but the exact location was only guesswork. The remainder of Company C left their patrol base in order to reinforce their platoon and SRP.

The Battalion Commander ordered Company B to move south of the perimeter and secure the ridgeline to cover Company C's withdrawal. Company C received harassing fire and sniper fire as they maneuvered through the dense jungle to assist the 2nd platoon and the SRP. The two groups combined their units at 2115 hours. The perimeter began receiving rounds soon after both units had merged. It was an intense fire barrage with many impacts occurring within the defensive positions. Task Force Swift directed artillery to place on the suspected enemy positions.

Throughout the night flashlights and NVA movements were observed continuously. At 0130 ours on March 12 seven to nine sets of headlights were observed southwest of Task Force Swift. Artillery was employed with undetermined results. At first light, patrols were sent out from the patrol base to search for signs of enemy movement. At 0810 hours the first platoon of Company B located the five men missing from the March 11th contact. The missing soldiers were evacuated and taken back to the patrol base perimeter. Airstrikes and artillery were employed on the enemy locations, killing 5 NVA. At 1350 hours another weapons attack was pointed at LZ Swinger, causing friendly casualties. At 1645 hours Task Force Swift received an intense array of mortars and small arms fire causing 15 WIA. This continued for 3 hours and ended at 1955 hours. Simultaneously LZ Swinger was again placed under heavy NVA bombardment by six 75 mm recoilless rifle rounds.

Artillery and airstrikes countered the enemy fire throughout the night. Friendly casualties for the day amounted to 10 soldiers killed (KIA) and 56 soldiers wounded (WIA). On March 13 LZ Swinger was again under bombardment by 82 mm mortar fire.

The Battalion commander knew that LZ Swinger needed additional manpower and support. He ordered Company A 3rd Battalion 12$^{th}$ Infantry to be airlifted to LZ Mary Lou and prepare for an assault on LZ Cider. In the meantime, Company A 1$^{st}$ Battalion 35$^{th}$ Infantry was airlifted from LZ Mary to secure LZ Swinger and provide additional support to the battered units. The wounded were extracted by the helicopters bringing Company A 1/35, along with the dead soldiers. The additional manpower was sorely needed and welcomed. But the relief was short lived. Harassing fire and mortars occurred throughout that night. Listening posts heard movements, and again observed flashlights, and some headlights moving along the trails. No further confrontations occurred that night.

Task Force Swift conducted the usual patrol sweeps with the third platoon of Company D finding 3 NVA killed in action (KIA) at 0845 hours along with one AK 47 rifle and documents. The second platoon observed a NVA reinforced bunker. The platoon leader ordered them to conduct an on-line attack against it. One squad moved and the other covered as they moved up the hill, and vice versa. The platoon received automatic weapons fire and RPG. They were able to direct their grenade launchers into it, silencing their weapons. The machine gun position was then captured, with the NVA quickly leaving down a trail. At 1215 hours the fourth platoon found a trail with markings of truck tire tracks. Sniper fire began harassing them and stopping their progress. They quickly regrouped and directed fire against the sniper position, killing the sniper. Then later that afternoon the third platoon found 2 more NVA killed. The day ended with 2 more soldiers from Task Force Swift killed (KIA). NVA losses were 8 dead.

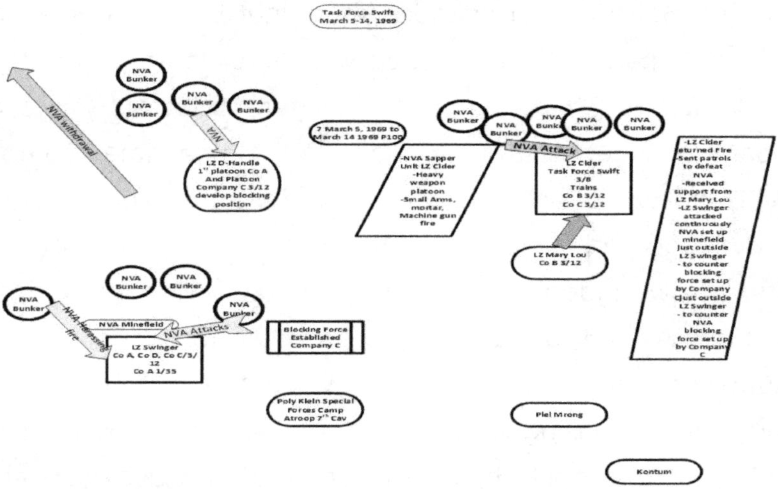


*Schematic Drawing 8—Task Force Swift*

Conversations took place and sounded like the following:

"6 Delta, this is 3 Delta. Found 3 NVA and1 AK47, plus documents. Will continue search on the trail," said the 3rd platoon leader, Company D.

"Roger that," said Company D Commander.

"6 Delta, this is 2 Delta. Found Bunkers at the top of the hill. We are attacking online assault toward the bunkers. Receiving fire." said the 2nd platoon leader of Company D.

“2 Delta, this is 6 Delta. Do you need support?” said the Company D Commander.

“6 Delta, this is 2 Delta. No, grenade launchers and our fire can overcome the bunkers. Snipers are shooting into our perimeter. Fire is now ceased from the bunkers and the sniper is silenced,” said the 2nd platoon leader of Company D.

”2 Delta, this is 6 Delta. Are there any casualties?” said the Company D Commander.

“6 Delta, this is 2 Delta. No casualties in taking the hill. Our reaction was swift and accurate,” said the 2nd platoon leader of Company D.

“2 Delta, this is 6 Delta. Way to go, carry on,” said the Company D Commander.

“6 Delta, this is 3 Delta. Found three more bunkers on the trail. Still searching, said the 3rd platoon leader of Company D.

“3 Delta, this is 6 Delta. Continue looking” said the Company D Commander.

# *Su Kotak Mountain Range*

Intelligence reports revealed that a NVA base camp was still the near objective LZ Brace . The brigade commander ordered TOC (Battalion Tactical Operations Center), CP (Command Post), Company D and B Battery, 6th Battalion, 29th Artillery to helicopter assault into LZ Cider and establish a fire support base. On March 14th, the engineers and Company A were transported to LZ Cider and commenced fire base construction. At 1841 hours LZ Swinger received the usual incoming on TOC (Tactical Operations Center), CP (Command Post), C Battery 1st Battalion 38th Artillery, and Company A 1st Battalion 35th Infantry. No casualties were incurred as a result of the incoming rounds. Company C and the first platoon of Company A were airlifted to LZ D-Handle to establish a fire support base for the 4.2 mortars and to place blocking positions along a NVA withdrawal route. At 1240 hours Company B initiated contact against a squad of NVA, killing one. For the next two days, outside the usual incoming pointed at LZ Swinger, there was no contact with unfriendly forces. Patrols again were sent out daily and found two bunker complexes, complete with linking tunnels, but abandoned. There were signs of recent inhabitance, but no signs of NVA presence. The patrol entered the tunnel to investigate and ensure no personnel were still left. No signs of activity were found outside of one pith helmet, one pair of sandals, and dressings with blood stains.

On March 19, a SRP 31(short range reconnaissance patrol) a part of the reconnaissance platoon, sighted one NVA soldier observing the platoon's claymore mines and defensive positions at a patrol base near LZ Cider. At the same time five additional NVA were sighted behind the NVA soldier who was observing the weapon positions. The SRP team reacted to this finding by directing small arms fire against them, blowing their claymore mines, and throwing fragmentation grenades toward them in order to withdraw to their perimeter. In their haste The Reconnaissance team left all of their equipment behind, and this included a radio. The Reconnaissance team made it safely into the perimeter. A later search of the area by the second platoon of Company A revealed fresh blood trails, the recovery of all abandoned equipment, and one NVA pith helmet bearing a bullet hole. No further contacts resulted in that area. The NVA team was a scouting party, and also had orders to disengage contact.

# Cadillac Hill

Also, on March 19th Company D was to attack Cadillac Hill. At 0910 hours members of the third platoon sighted one NVA soldier in a bunker complex. After adjusting over 40 rounds of 82mm mortar rounds on the location the third platoon leader advanced toward the bunker complex. The platoon immediately encountered sniper fire but continued to move towards the objective. At 1022 hours they met a platoon size force (about 30 men) that was well-entrenched on the top of Cadillac Hill.

The platoon leader ordered his men to withdraw to allow fire support to assist them in their attack. NVA mortar fire began to fall near the third platoon, hampering withdrawal efforts and forcing the platoon members to seek cover and wait for reinforcements. Yet even after an airstrike and over four hundred rounds of artillery pounded Cadillac Hill, the NVA still remained in force and continued to place deadly fire on the platoon.

The second platoon of Company D moved to the contact site, and at 1053 hours began receiving small arms fire from a squad of NVA (about 8 men) that was strategically placed between the two platoons. This prevented the platoons from joining forces. The enemy force was small, but the two platoons were unable to maneuver around them until later that afternoon when it closed to within 75 meters of the third platoon. Shouts between the two platoons were the only means of communication. The third platoon leader, who was severely wounded as well as many of his platoon wounded or killed, rallied the able-bodied troops, and reorganized them to link with the second platoon. However, the NVA squad continued to fire mortars into the third platoon; and then it adjusted its fire on the second platoon's location causing immediate casualties. The battalion commander ordered the two platoons to move east about 400 meters to evacuate the wounded at a landing zone area. Most of the third platoon was able to join the 2nd platoon by 1800 hours, and both were able to make a successful withdrawal to their patrol base. Stragglers from the third platoon including the platoon leader conducted a successful escape and evasion from the enemy and managed to close the perimeter around 1800 hours. No further movement from the hostile force was detected after that time until the next evening.

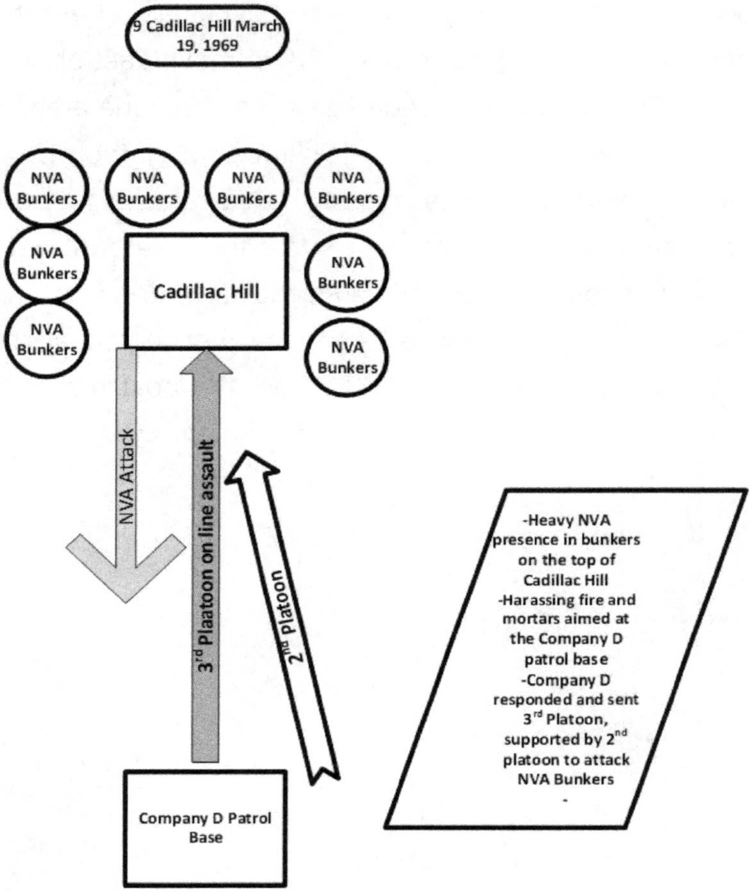


*Schematic Drawing 9—Cadillac Hill*

The Medevac helicopters were able to extract the wounded. A resupply Helicopter dropped off ammunition and supplies, then removed the dead soldiers. The platoons suffered a high rate of casualties from this encounter. The total number of casualties from both was 4 killed in action (KIA), 19 wounded in action (WIA), and 3 missing in action (MIA). A search was conducted for the missing soldiers, but with no success.

The numbers of NVA killed in action were 7 KIA and an unknown number that were wounded.

"Spooky" was employed to spray the surrounding area with heavy 50mm machine gun fire. "Spooky" was the nickname given to an older model Caribou that was equipped with 50 caliber machine guns, whose role was to place fire on suspected enemy locations. The fire was deadly and accurate. In addition, the platoons directed artillery fire on Cadillac Hill throughout the night. Listening posts placed outside the patrol base noted movement close to their perimeter.

The next day LZ Cider was probed on March 19 with small arms fire; Airstrikes and artillery fire were placed on the enemy suspected locations. One NVA soldier was killed in action. Company D's attack on Cadillac Hill was postponed because of fog and the inability of the Air Force to provide timely assault preparatory fire on the objective.

On March 20 heavy artillery and mortar fire were placed on LZ Cider. Company D attempted their attack at 0825 hours and were directed to recover their missing in action during their previous assault. At 1000 hours Company D reached the contact site and recovered two men's bodies. They were confronted with small arms fire, Machine gun fire, and B-40 rockets from the indestructible bunker complex. The Company Commander ordered his platoon to pull back and directed artillery and gunships on the bunker complex. For the next two hours the bombardment continued.

*Figure 22 Cobra Gun Ship*

At 1225 hours Company D advanced toward the objective with 7th Battalion, 17th Air Cavalry Division screening their element. Forward movement was halted again at 1518 hours by small arms fire, B-40 rockets, and automatic weapons. Artillery and gunships were placed on the objective, enabling Company D to withdraw to their base without interference. Artillery and gunships continued to strike Cadillac Hill until 1729 hours. Airstrikes continued throughout that evening. The NVA regrouped their strengths and began an indirect fire attack on LZ Cider. For 40 minutes, 100 rounds of 82 mm mortars as well as 75mm recoilless rifle rounds impacted within the perimeter. To counter the NVA attack on the landing zone, the 105 howitzer and 4.2 mm mortars directed their fire on the objective. This stopped the ongoing attack of LZ Cider, at least temporarily. Nevertheless, at 2315 hours the NVA focused their mortars and small arms fire at LZ Cider penetrating the perimeter's bunkers. The commanding officer ordered airstrikes on the location of the NVA and employed artillery and 4.2 mortars on all known and suspected NVA locations that night and into the next day. Movement was noted by listening posts located outside of LZ Cider and LZ D-Handle.

On March 22, the Air Force coordinated their bombardment with Company D's assault on the objective Cadillac Hill. This time the NVA had disappeared, and no return fire was encountered. Later, an ambush patrol of Company C observed the sighting of three NVA soldiers. They engaged the three soldiers and eliminated them. It appeared these soldiers were the last ones to be present in the area of Cadillac Hill, and they were probably left to harass the remaining forces. The main unit withdrew to regroup. Sporadic incidents of ground to air fire against resupply helicopters continued around LZ Cider. Company D found four NVA killed in action in the bunker complex.

On March 27 the third platoon of Company A while moving northwest on a trail to follow a mortar and artillery preparation fire, observed 4 NVA soldiers moving toward them. They initiated contact, killing 2 NVA soldier . Then as the platoon advanced on the other two, an intense mortar barrage, small arms fire, B-40 rockets, and automatic weapons raked into the platoon. The platoon leader reorganized his forces and ordered the unit to withdraw to allow artillery and gunships to expend on the bunker complex. The platoon began moving to the rear, encountering heavy and intense fire from the sides and the rear, killing the platoon leader. This splits the platoon into two groups. One group consisted of dead and seriously wounded personnel. The other consisted of ambulatory wounded and those not wounded. The latter group managed to move 200 meters southeast of the contact site. The platoon sergeant who was located in the second group called for the remaining two platoons to assist them in withdrawing. The NVA continued to fire into the unit. Artillery fire did not seem to damage the bunkers. Airstrikes were ruled out due to the nearness of the platoons to the enemy location. Company A's progress was hampered by sporadic sniper and mortar fire. After five hours of trudging toward its third platoon they finally were able to join it and assisted in the evacuation of the wounded. Company A was unable to reach the contact site to retrieve the wounded and dead because of the intense automatic weapons and mortar fire. The Company A Commander ordered his men to withdraw to their patrol base and closed at 2025 hours. Hasty, stay-behind ambushes were set up, but with no results. Artillery and mortar fire continued throughout the night on the bunker/trench complex location.

On March 28, 1969, Company A again moved out to the contact site and immediately was subjected to intense automatic weapons, small arms, and mortar fire. The NVA was estimated to be a platoon-sized force (about 30 men). At 1330 hours the Battalion Commander ordered Company A to withdraw. Their evacuation was supported by a thunderous volume of artillery and mortar fire. Gunships also expended on the enemy locations, providing further covering fire. Once Company A reached the patrol base perimeter, the Company Commander directed air strikes and artillery on the bunker complex. Later that afternoon, the SRP (Short range Reconnaissance Platoon) from Company D observed five NVA soldiers passing by their location. 82 mm mortar fire was directed on the newly found bunkers. However, the NVA sensed that the forward observer was close to their location and began to advance on the SRP location and split into two groups. 20 meters from the SRP's location the NVA soldiers concealed themselves behind fallen trees. Mortars continued to fire on the suspected enemy locations in support of the SRP. When darkness came the NVA began moving toward the SRP location. The SRP detonated their claymore mines, adjusted the artillery fire to within 20 meters of their location, and broke contact by moving toward their perimeter LZ D-Handle through dense jungle and rugged terrain. The NVA followed them close behind. One of the men tripped and fell, slowing the movement. An NVA soldier came up to the SRP. Quickly, the team engaged him by hitting him in the head, knocking him unconscious. They then were able to continue their movement back to the patrol base. Two NVA again followed them but were unable to catch up to them. Finally, the SRP reached the perimeter.

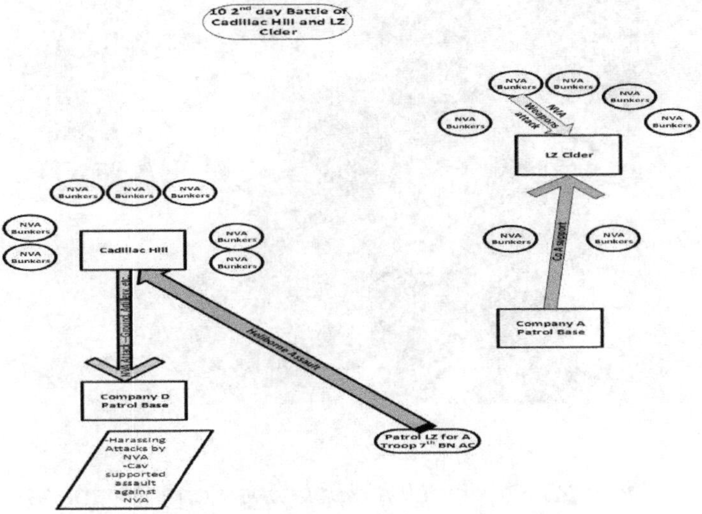


*Schematic Drawing 10—Second Day of Battle for Cadillac Hill*

# LZ D-Handle

The SRP's contact alerted LZ D-Handle's perimeter to the possibility of a ground attack. But the perimeter grew lax as the NVA unit failed to come immediately after the SRP entered the perimeter. The surprise had been compromised, and the NVA did not pursue. Since the anticipated attack did not occur, an alert was disregarded. At 0555 Hours March 29 a listening post guard was found asleep by an NVA sapper, who stealthily killed him and motioned other sappers that the perimeter was ripe for a sapper attack.

*Figure 23 Sapper Unit displaying Long Weapons filled with explosives*

The sapper directed mortar fire on LZ D-Handle and began attacking with the pole and satchel charges to breach the perimeter by surprise. The men quickly regrouped and reacted immediately to begin close hand to hand combat fighting to repel the sappers. In less than ten minutes after the fighting began, the sappers withdrew, leaving behind a disaster—2 US soldiers KIA, and 28 WIA. Nevertheless, the quick reaction by Company D resulted in the deaths of 3 NVA sappers.

At 1130 hours the second platoon of Company B engaged an enemy squad killing one NVA soldier and one Viet Cong. Sporadic sniper fire continued throughout the day and at 2000 hours LZ D-Handle began receiving mortar fire. The 82 mm mortars impacted in the perimeter for about forty-five minutes at every 10-minute intervals. Fortunately, the men were able to protect themselves by being in fortified bunkers. The firing from mortars finally stopped, and the unit regrouped.

The NVA incurred heavy losses in attacking LZ D-Handle. At 1115 hours in spite of this, a small unit attacked a listening post. The men returned fire and repelled the attack. One NVA soldier was killed in action. At 1431 hours Company A moved toward a bunker complex to recover the bodies of the eight missing in action soldiers from their previous engagement. The company reached the contact site at 1525 hours in spite of sporadic sniper fire. It then moved toward their objective. At 1720 hours and platoon-sized force-initiated contact with the lead platoon only one hundred fifty meters from the objective, causing casualties. The company commander ordered his men to withdraw. The NVA responded to the withdrawal by attacking the Company with mortars, automatic weapons fire, RPG (rifle propelled grenades) , and small arms fire (AK47). The company withdrew to a hillside, where it reminded until 1900 hours. (It was important to seek the high ground to defend themselves.) Enemy sniper fire continued to harass their positions. Company C was moved to support Company A in the withdrawal process.

Both Company A and C combined forces at 1900 hours and returned to the perimeter at LZ D-Handle at 2000 hours. At 0035 hours Company A and C received incoming rounds from mortars, small arms, machine guns, and B-40 rockets. This continued to the early morning hours.

On March 31 both units were extracted to LZ Cider from their patrol base. Ground to air contact from the entrenched enemy hampered extraction efforts. However, the sorties were successful in making the extraction. LZ Cider also received seven rounds of mixed mortar and recoilless rifle rounds without casualties. LZ D-Handle experienced thirty-five rounds of mixed 82mm and 60 mm mortar fire, causing three US soldiers to be wounded in action. Artillery and airstrikes were employed on enemy positions throughout the day and into the next night.

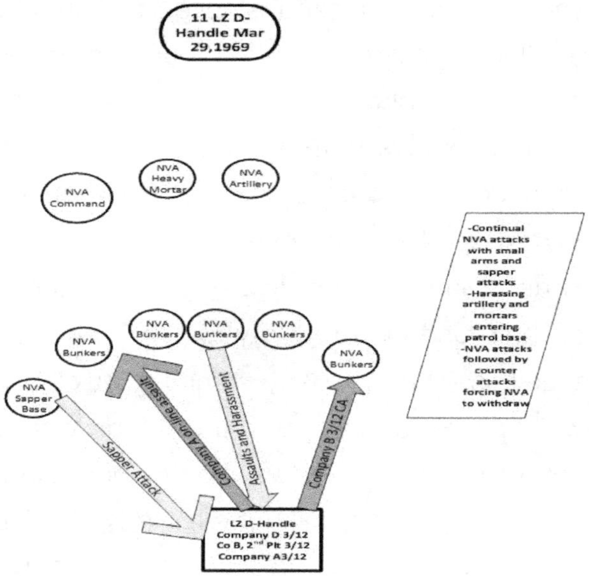


*Schematic Drawing 11-LZ D-Handle*

## Summary of the Plei Trap Valley Operation

The Plei Trap Valley involved three significant operations, each of which resulted in the infliction of severe casualties and equipment losses on the enemy. Infiltration routes were blocked, and enemy strongholds were destroyed. The continuous enemy bombardment of LZ Swinger, the harassing sniper fire on LZ Cider, and the battles of LZ Swinger, LZ Brace, Hill 800, and LZ D-Handle caused many casualties on both sides. All of the battles were fought in a conventional manner, for each side used extensive artillery preparation prior to the attack. The NVA's attack on Kontum province and Polei Kleng was halted by an aggressive, determined, combined forces which completely disrupted a base area and prevented major enemy attacks in Kontum Province. Task Force Swift was effective by minimizing the NVA effectiveness in Kontum province.

## Spring Campaign 1969

After the Plei Trap Valley campaign, the Battalion received a long stand down. On May 1, 1969, the 3rd Battalion 12th Infantry began another operation east of An Khe. For the next two weeks no NVA or Viet Cong forces were spotted or engaged. The Battalion was then ordered to search and clear an area south of highway 19 near "VC Valley" a former stronghold. The Viet Cong placed harassing fires on the patrol bases on three occasions, but these passed without casualties. One VC (Viet Cong) was found dead from the counter-mortar fire placed on suspected unfriendly locations.

# Search of the Rocket Box

With intelligence reports indicating that 122mm Rocket attacks were imminent against Pleiku City, the battalion began saturation patrolling an area commonly referred to as the "Rocket Box". It is located about ten kilometers west of Pleiku City, an area that is mostly populated by Montagnard of which most of them were considered unfriendly. On May 18 Company D received six rounds of 60mm mortar fire at 1550 hours. The fire was countered by artillery and mortar fire. Patrol sweeps the next day provided information about new VC trails and newly built hooches.

On the morning of May 20th another sweep of the Plei Yoi area was conducted. Villages were searched and located five persons of questionable status. The objective was to locate Viet Cong in the villages. After intensive interrogation one person admitted he was the village director of B-5 village, B-4 District, and Viet Gia Lai Province, Viet Cong. Further questioning revealed that there was an arms cache nearby.

On May 21 the third platoon of Company B combined with the first platoon A Troop, 1st Squad 10th Air Cavalry to search for the alleged arms caches. As the point element neared the cache location, a NVA unit (about 200 men), hidden in well-entrenched bunkers and caves, initiated contact, and caused light casualties. The platoon leader reorganized his platoon and rallied them against the NVA unit. Artillery and gunships were called to direct fire on the bunker and cave complex. For five hours intense fire was exchanged with the NVA. Finally, the contact was broken at 1540 hours. After the battle ended Air Cavalry observers stated that 96 NVA had died in the action.

## Plei Preng Het and the Cordon

Sporadic contacts with small forces dominated operations until June 22 when an ambush patrol from Company B engaged a NVA squad. The NVA returned fire wounding one US soldier and then withdrew to the north. The unit was pursued until they disappeared into the thick foliage. For the next four days light action was reported.

On June 26 at 1520 hours the first platoon of Company D observed fifteen NVA on a trail. The patrol reacted quickly and initiated contact, killing four of them. Patrols continued without any significant findings until June 30 when Company D came upon the village of Plei Preng Het. It was believed that the fifteen NVA spotted on June 26th were located in village. The Company commander strategized with his platoon leaders as to the best way to bring them out in the open so that they could kill or capture them. The platoons were deployed in four directions to surround the village. This in effect formed a cordon, from which the NVA could not escape. Artillery was ruled out because it could not be used when villagers may be intermingled with them. Stealthily the platoons set up and as the cordon was being completed the NVA attempted to evade detection and run from the village. When they attempted to pass the cordon claymore mines were blown, and automatic weapons and small arms fire were directed at them. All fifteen NVA continued to flee. Not one of them surrendered. The cordon though stopped their progress and the platoons exchanged fire with them, killing all fifteen soldiers. There were no friendly casualties in the encounter. The NVA did not want to be captured and fought to the death. During the battle, it was discovered that these soldiers tied themselves with rope so that none of them could escape. They decided to make a stand against Company D. It looked as if several had committed suicide as well. The men buried the NVA soldiers after the contact ended. The company commander and the platoon leaders could not believe what they saw. Documents and weapons were recovered from the dead NVA.

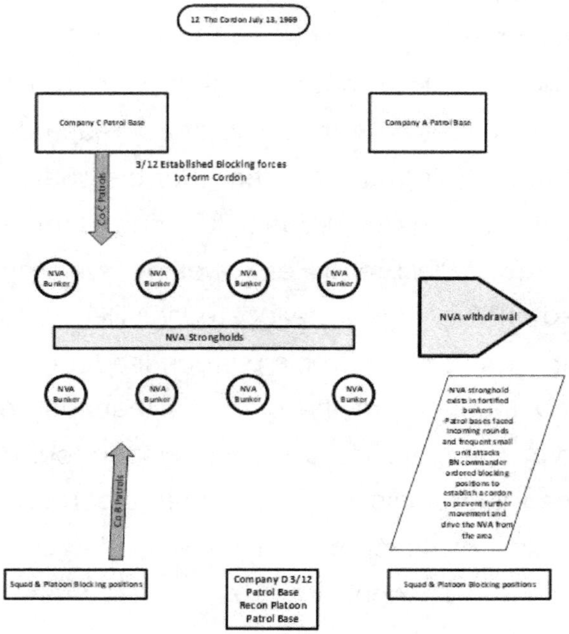

# Battles South of An Khe and Camp Radcliffe

No major action occurred until July 13. A platoon-sized force-initiated contact on the lead element of the reconnaissance platoon, resulting in 3 friendly KIA (killed in action) and 1 WIA (wounded in action) . The platoon leader was one of the ones killed in action. The platoon sergeant reorganized the platoon and directed them to place fire on the NVA positions. Gunships were called in for support and directed rockets and automatic weapons fire on them to cover the recovery efforts by the platoon to remove the wounded and dead. In turn, the NVA fired their weapons toward the helicopters as well and at the embattled platoon, hampering the efforts to pick up the wounded soldier and remove the dead soldiers. The helicopter managed to take on only a few of the wounded and had to leave due to the heavy fire. The platoon sergeant rallied his troops and brought them into a tight circle to offer more protection against the fire. He radioed the battalion commander for reinforcements to cover the withdrawal.

Company D was ordered to combat assault into the contact area. They moved from the landing zone to the contact area and entered the patrol's perimeter. In the meantime, at 1122 hours, Company A established a blocking position north of the contact site. The blocking position was to prevent further NVA infiltration into the area that would reinforce the engaged force. Sporadic sniper fire continuously penetrated the remaining members of the platoon. Company A began receiving mortar and small arms fire. Artillery and mortars continued to support withdrawal efforts of the platoon. An airstrike was placed on the NVA positions. Finally, after four hours of continuous engagement, the contact was broken, and the wounded and dead were transported to Company A's location.

Throughout that afternoon and evening movement by an unknown-sized force was detected around the contact area. The patrol's perimeter was probed during the night. At 1100 hours Company C was airlifted to a landing northeast of the contact site. Company D then established blocking positions to form a cordon to prevent further NVA infiltration. At 1318 hours Company C, pushing toward Company A's positions, observed soldiers moving toward Company A. They were engaged, and they quickly withdrew back into heavy foliage. At 1730 hours the first platoon of Company D engaged the NVA soldiers that were spotted earlier. One NVA soldier was confirmed killed in action. There were no friendly casualties. The Battalion Commander believed that the NVA had withdrawn from the area and that remnants of the main force remained to harass and hinder movement of the companies to search for NVA locations. His thoughts were confirmed through intelligence reports. He felt that the mission had been completed He ordered a battalion stand down in order to receive reinforcements and a much-needed rest at Camp Radcliffe at An Khe.

# Operation Ridge Runner—Search for 95th NVA Regiment

Enemy activity increased along Highway 19 and in the Mang Yang Pass region. Highway 19 ran from Qui Nhon to An Khe to Pleiku City and beyond to the Cambodia border. It was the main resupply route for the Central Highlands. It was a key highway, and the control of the highway was a definite advantage for the armies involved.

***Figure 24 Deuce and Half Truck on Convoy duty on Highway 19***

The French in 1954 were nearly wiped out on the Mang Yang Pass defending the highway against a strongly entrenched enemy force. The French lost this battle undertaking heavy casualties. Not being able to control the movement of supplies on the highways hampered further efforts to secure the road. The French were forced to withdraw. As a result of that battle and for other reasons the French withdrew from Vietnam.

Convoys were again being harassed along highway 19. The NVA unit suspected of conducting this activity was the 95th NVA regiment. There were many intelligence reports that indicated that the regiment was relocating to the Mang Yang Pass area. The topography of the area was rugged and extremely hilly. Mountains were interspersed with multiple hills. Triple canopy jungle occupied the mountainsides and valleys limiting visibility. This provided excellent cover for the NVA regiment. Movements were invisible by observers, as they were well concealed. Once in a while villager did notify the Vietnamese government of enemy locations, but most of that information was never passed onto the American units in the area.

The 3rd Battalion, 12th Infantry was ordered to begin a search and destroy operation along the rugged ridgelines and valleys south of Highway 19 between An Khe and the Mang Yang Pass. On August 1, the battalion was transported by convoy to LZ Action and then air lifted to LZ Joan to commence operations.

This was my first involvement with the unit. A letter to home describes the initial entrance to this part of the war.

*"Hi all,*

*The battalion is located in the picturesque mountain region about 50 km east of Pleiku. There are no inhabitants in this area, and all persons found here are considered "free targets." Sleep at Headquarters of the Battalion is constantly interrupted by howitzers and 4.2 mortars. Last night the Headquarters received about sixty incoming rounds from an unknown VC location. They were expected to gain strength in September and October.*

*All is not as difficult as it sounds. Life in a compound is tense, but there is time for relaxation, at least for those in the Headquarters area.*

*Company D is engaged in an overall search and destroy mission. Patrols, both night and day, cover about ten square kilometers or what we call 10 clicks square on a military map.*

*Helicopter operations take place often, but patrols are mostly forced marches up and down shaggy, steep cliffs. The air in the mountains is cool at night, warm during the day. It is highly malaria infested here. We see few snakes and monkeys on or near the trails. It is full of strange sounds of birds, insects, and jungle animals. The dirt is red and is caked on our clothes. Water flowing in streams looks pure and clean, but it is not and requires tablets. However, some of us have run out of them and take our chances.*

*I will write more about it when I can.*

*LTD"*

For the first three weeks Patrols were operating on the top of ridges and down the hills in triple canopy jungle areas. The men referred to it as the "hump" and placed "Operation Ridge Runner" in ink on the top of their helmets. Abundant food supplies and recently built huts (commonly referred to as "hooches") were found. These were made of straw. Some were on stilts, others just stored items like a shed. Pigs and chickens surrounded these huts. They were located in areas that were considered uninhabitable. This gave some indication that there were a sizable number of persons requiring these necessities. Booby traps and trip wires often were in the "hooches" that added peril to searching them. Spear traps were placed along trails, and even more sophisticated traps put in place by the Viet Cong. Some of the traps found were a tiger pit lined with pungi sticks that was camouflaged. When a unit was on the trail, the trap was not detected very easily. Personnel would go through to the pungi sticks below causing significant injury and a requirement for a "Dust Off" (Medevac or the Medical helicopter to pick up a wounded soldier and take them to a medical facility). Others found included the placement of spikes in a tree, and a trap to pick up a soldier and slam him against the tree with wooden spikes, also causing injury. Montagnard Viet Cong also armed themselves with poison arrows. They would shoot them from a cross bow. These would cause infection and injury. Of course, because of the heavy brush and jungle, movement and detection were exceedingly difficult to locate.

During the mission, a green 2nd lieutenant was airlifted into a patrol base during the "hump". His assignment was to take over the 2nd platoon of Company D, 3d Bn. 12th Inf. He was nicknamed "LTD." The platoon leader he faced was LTP, a red headed grizzly faced 1st Lieutenant who had spent one year as a combat platoon leader. He was going back to the "world" ("World" referred back to the normal life in the States) in three days and was looking forward to being relieved by this greenhorn. LTP took a lot of time introducing LTD to his platoon. There were 21 in the field today. Each one had a nickname. Some only were referred to with their last name. LTD was introduced to "quick finger" (machine gunner), RTO (Radio Telephone Operator of the PRC 25) , "slick" (the usual point man), Burk (the sergeant who just turned 20), Ganes (a grunt or infantry soldier), Petey, (another grunt), and then the rest of the crew (all grunts and two grenade carriers) plus a medic called "Doc". Each talked about how many days they had left. Of course, LTD had 361 days left, and LTP had 3. Most of the others had over 180 days left, except Petey who had 35. The next morning the "chopper" (helicopter) arrived and LTP bid goodbye. LTD was on his own with his platoon. Fortunately for him, there was little contact in the area, and this made it easier to assimilate into the platoon. What LTD did not expect was the weight of the ruck sack that carried the poncho, jungle blanket, two weeks of "C" rations, 5 magazines of M16 bullets, three hand grenades, and 4 sticks of C-4 explosives along with the fuse wire. The can opener became a coveted tool to survive to open the cans. The weight of the ruck sack was 92 lbs. LTD only weighed 135 lbs. Once during the "hump" LTD tripped and because of the ***weight*** on his back, he rolled down the hill, much to the laughter of his platoon. It was a lighter moment to be remembered.

During the maneuvers traps were encountered One incident occurred as follows. The 2nd platoon of Company D was searching along a trail. The movement was single file. It was a typical day for a "walk in the woods", which meant that the attention on any enemy activity was just cursory. Nothing was expected. The platoon leader LTD was in the point element. Suddenly, a string was noticed by the point. His hand went up to stop the column. The platoon leader came up to him. As he was moving forward his foot went underneath the string and tripped the spear. For some reason it missed the platoon leader and stuck into a tree near the trail. The spear went about three inches into the tree, showing what force it had when it was sprung. LTD was lucky this time, as the spear just graze his leg on its movement. The platoon stopped and the order to search the area for other traps was given. The platoon was split into four squads to cover all four directions. When one of the squads came around large boulder, another also came around the other side. Each pulled its weapon thinking the other was a VC. Fortunately, the two stopped before the trigger was pulled. They recognized each other. The reaction was from the extensive training they both received on engaging a target. It could have been a disastrous encounter.

Small units were deployed to search for NVA and Viet Cong in the area. Numerous small contacts occurred, but no major contacts. Most of them were a hit and run type contact.

In one of the contacts with the Viet Cong, the second platoon of Company D was again walking the ridgeline in a single file column. At 1400 hours, the point element noticed a movement along the hillside. LTD had the platoon get into a defensive position and took a small element to find out what the movement was. As they were going on the trail a sniper bullet was fired above their heads, not wounding any member of the unit. The element fired back at the direction of the sniper's bullet. Then they went to investigate and found no remnants of the sniper. The VC sniper disappeared quickly and stealthily. This type of contact occurred weekly and sometimes daily. The VC blended into the landscape. The platoon moved onward down the trail and located a small village. They searched it and found no evidence of any Viet Cong in the village. The VC sniper assimilated in the village. It was difficult to get the townspeople to point out a VC member or sympathizer to a military unit.

The companies walked over fifty days on the tops of the ridgelines. Often, resupply was impossible due to heavy fog and monsoon rains. As a result, food supplies were short for units on patrols. There were no roads where the troops could be resupplied by convoy. Often the patrols stopped searching for VC, and instead searched for food. Even the bark off the trees was able to be eaten as protein. Some of the food eaten instead of "C" rations were jungle rats, snake, monkey, fruits such as pineapple, and others as well as plants and wild vegetables. Due to the constant rain fires were difficult to maintain so much of what was eaten was cold. Insects were also eaten. Clothes could not be exchanged, so the troops often wore the same uniform for weeks. The feet took a toll because they were always wet. This caused what is referred to as "jungle rot" or sores on legs and feet that seem to grow daily. Once in a great while when "hooches" were found deserted, there were chickens and pigs that were foraged and given to the troops. This was a feast! Then, after receiving the unusual food for energy to move forward, the patrols searched for more Viet Cong in the area. It seemed as if there were more monkeys than VC, and the search was often. Also, it seemed as if the approach of the troops in an area was well communicated, and the VC disappeared into the jungle to fight another day.

Each company was tasked physically as well as being frustrated with the lack of action and the strenuous hump along the ridgeline. The Viet Cong and the NVA were elusive, and no signs of them could be found. Artillery fire was directed on suspected locations, with no known results. During this operation there were few incidents of harassment along highway 19 and as a result, the operation was declared a success. In August and September, Highway 19 had a significant reduction in ambushes on convoys, attacks on villages, and destroyed bridges. With its mission fulfilled, the battalion was evacuated and airlifted to Camp Radcliffe for a stand down waiting for the next assignment. The 95th NVA regiment was believed to have moved south.

# Operation Punchbowl

On October 19, 1969, the 3d Battalion, 12th Infantry began a road march from Camp Radcliffe, An Khe City, Binh Dinh Province, and along highway 19 to Plei Djereng air strip. Small enemy forces placed harassing fire on the huge convoy, causing one minor casualty. Preceding the convoy was a tank unit which fired on both sides of the road to clear it of potential VC or NVA activity. It was nicknamed "Thunder Road," as the big guns from the tanks sounded like thunder. Mines in the road were discovered on three occasions and disarmed by an infantry soldier so that the convoy could continue. This slowed down the pace of the convoy. The tanks moved forward with infantry soldiers riding on the outside of the tank. Also among the tanks were APC (armed personnel carriers) which carried additional troops. The rest of the convoy carried supplies, ammunition, weapons, food, shelter, and troops. The tanks gave the convoy a peace of mind as they were all sure that if there were any insurgents lurking along the road that the tank fire would eliminate them. After eleven hours traveling the battalion reached the air strip at 1900 hours.

The brigade commander and his command staff received intelligence reports indicating a large NVA presence in the Plei Djereng area. The air strip was continuously receiving 122 mm rocket fire, and observation helicopter received small arms and machine gun fire as they traveled throughout the region. Along with the ARVN commander, a joint operation was developed with the ARVN army pushing South and the 3d battalion, 12th infantry serving as a blocking force to stop the infiltration and NVA movement in the area. The NVA were considered heavily armed, and there was evidence of heavy artillery being transported in the region. Chinese advisors had been spotted by a special force's unit operating in the area, along with several Chinese operated helicopters. There were also unsubstantiated reports of MIG jets flying overhead into Cambodia. This was going to be a difficult mission and with contact.

At 0600 hours the next day all units of Company A and the 1st platoon, 4th engineering battalion were airlifted into LZ Delta to prepare a fire support base and the TAC CP (Tactical Command Post commonly referred to as TOC) area. At 1458 hours, sniper fire was observed at the Plei Djereng air strip. No casualties were reported, or sorties (helicopters) hit. Observation airplanes parked there to help direct air strikes along the front also avoided being hit. These planes were referred to as the "Pregnant Pelican" because the nose of the airplane was clear Plexiglas so that a forward observer could be sitting there and be able to see 360 degrees over the ground. It gave him an unobstructed vision and also enabled him to direct the pilot to move to a closer view of suspected activity. The pilot then radioed the air force command tower if a bombing mission was needed, and type of bombs+ it required. Of course, these planes were often targeted by the VC or NVA.

On October 21 Company B conducted a combat assault from the Plei Djereng airfield into the Chu Pa Mountains and established a patrol base. Both Company C and D conducted a Heliborne (movement by helicopters) assault into a landing zone that required a ten-to-twenty-foot leap to the ground. At 1700 hours Company D experienced their first tragedy when a helicopter hit a tree when landing, crashed, killing 2 soldiers, and injuring four others. The accident delayed the incoming helicopters until the landing zone was cleared. A Medevac helicopter came and removed the wounded. Once the helicopter wreck was cleared by the unit, the landings continued until all of the troops landed without incident. (It was a COLD LZ.) The company secured the area that night to commence operations the next morning. Listening posts (LP's) were started as well as patrols to explore the area and search for NVA presence.

*Figure 25 Infantryman on Maneuvers*

The next two days the companies conducted local patrols without results. Company C Listening Post's heard movement on both nights. Artillery was employed with unknown results. At 2100 hours the battalion trains located at LZ Oasis was subjected to a 122 mm rocket attack with direct hits on an artillery tent and medical tent. Sniper fire was also encountered at the LZ Oasis. One soldier was seriously wounded in the action. The NVA incoming rocket fire was countered with artillery.

On October 23, the ARVN (ARMY REPUBLIC OF VIETNAM) regiment began sweeping south toward the blocking positions of the 3d battalion 12th infantry, and established patrol bases for their night locations. On the next day, the push by ARVN toward the blocking position flushed the NVA between the two elements, forcing them to make contact. At 0843 hours on October 24 the third platoon of Company D was engaged by a small aggressive squad of about 8 NVA soldiers who initiated contact with its point element, killing one US soldier and wounding another. The 3rd platoon leader directed his platoon to fire back against them. The platoon moved aggressively against the NVA squad, forcing them to withdraw. In fact, the platoon leader stated that he found cover by being behind a six-inch diameter tree. That gave him the confidence to begin an attack and directly confront the hostile force. The aggressiveness shown by this platoon frightened the NVA so much that they dropped two of their weapons and three magazines in their flight. The first platoon of Company D joined the 3rd platoon and conducted a search and clear operation to seek the enemy. One B-40 rocket, and one magazine were found during the sweep, but no other presence of an enemy force was observed or confronted. That night, the sound of shovels and metal clanging against stone were heard in the patrol base. The sounds appeared to be in all directions. The patrol base was probed by rocks and flares, but no engagement occurred. Some thought it was an orangutan that was throwing objects into the perimeter, but that was quickly dispelled. NVA presence was near.

Other sightings were reported. The first of which was made by the battalion commander who spotted a radio antenna from his helicopter that was flying above the operations. Company D, while on a search of the area, was dispatched around that location to determine its significance, but the antenna was not found. At 1030 hours the reconnaissance platoon found three freshly made bunkers with overhead cover. The bunkers had been inhabited recently as fresh food and supplies were found. Both of these findings and the day's contact were proof that the enemy force was located between the 3rd Battalion, 12th Infantry and the ARVN 42nd regiment. Along with the observations made by the commander and those made by visual reconnaissance, intelligence personnel surmised on October 25 that because of the sixteen NVA initiated contacts recorded in the Pleiku/ Kontum Provinces that a concentration of NVA forces in this area was most likely occurring. They forecasted that the NVA would increase their presence over the next seven days. The targets included LZ Weight Davis, LZ Black Hawk, highway 19 from Pleiku to An Khe, LZ Oasis, Camp Enari, Pleiku, Toah-canh, Plei Mrong, highway 14 between Kontum and Pleiku, LZ Mary Lou, Kontum City, Dak To, and Ben Het Special Forces Camp. Because of the added information, all 4th Division units were to maintain a 2/3 alert and take precautionary measures against an attack.

Due to the warnings and intelligence briefings on the NVA increases of their unit sizes, the battalion continued conducting patrols around their patrol bases and increased guard presence during the evening hours. At 1145 hours the first platoon, Company B, found a massive 100 bunker complex with mess bunkers, storage areas, and a medical facility in it. It was estimated to be less than a year old. Paths, well-worn, all started from the circular perimeter. It reminded the platoon of a bicycle spoke. The paths all started from the center and went in all directions from the center.

At 1455 hours the first platoon of Company D located a freshly made bunker complex about 800 meters northeast of Company B's findings. At 1700 hours the battalion commander flying an observation mission in his light observation helicopter received ground to air fire. It was a sophisticated anti-aircraft fire that just missed him. He also received some sporadic automatic weapons fire from the ground.

That evening and into the next day, intelligence reports from observers and on the ground and in the air believed a regiment-sized force (about 500 NVA) was present near the battalion's blocking positions. More digging noises were heard that night. The next morning the third platoon of Company C observed NVA soldiers with pith helmets on three separate occasions. Each time artillery and gunships were directed to engage them, but with unknown results.

On October 28, the joint operation with the 42nd ARVN Regiment ended as the artillery was moved from LZ Delta to LZ Bravo. This move vacated the blocking position that was forcing them to be between both units. It also meant the loss of some artillery support. The move of the ARVN unit was unexpected, and the brigade commander had a new strategy to put in place. The battalion was to be the aggressor and search for NVA and destroy them. He felt that the aggressive moves would compromise the NVA position and deter them from further contacts. Patrols were increased, and B52 bombers were to place bombs at night on suspected positions. Later in the evening hours, Snoopy was also to fly over NVA positions and direct fire. Artillery and F104 phantom jets were also on call to support the company units. Movement was detected by each company during the night.

# Battle of the Streambed

On October 29 at 0845 hours the radio relay team observed two NVA scouts moving down a trail near their location. At 0945 hours a squad from Company C initiated contact with four NVA soldiers. After a sweep of the contact area, one NVA soldier body and one AK47 rifle was found along the trail. Other blood trails were spotted, but further searches did not reveal any more sign of NVA. Simultaneously, the second platoon of Company B, containing the Company Commander was moving northwest of their patrol base to search for arms caches near a streambed. What the company commander did not know is that the NVA had fortified bunker positions at the top of the hill so that they had an advantage in their field of fire down to the streambed. Snipers climbed trees in preparation of a contact near the hill. "Spider holes" were dug at the base of the hill to conceal soldiers waiting to ambush an oncoming unit. B-40 rockets and automatic weapons positions were put in place. The bunker complex was then stocked with mortar rounds and mortars, as well as RPG (rifle propelled grenades, and recoilless rifles.

Due to the dense undergrowth, all of these activities were concealed and could not be observed by aircraft.

Company B 2nd Platoon was spotted coming down the trail by an observation post. They fired their small arms weapons (AK47) into the unit, killing the point man. The observation post then quickly moved back to their perimeter and disengaged. However, the Company Commander and the Platoon Leader rallied their unit and ordered them to return fire. They did not have time to grieve over the loss of the soldier. The platoon aggressively moved toward the NVA bunkers. As they moved, sniper fire hampered any movement forward. The platoon leader was mortally wounded by a B-40 rocket. He gallantly tried to direct his troops to fight and assault the NVA positions, even after he was fatally wounded. With the platoon leader down, the Company Commander gathered the remainder of his troops and directed them to place fire on the bunkers and sniper positions. The NVA increased their volume of small arms fire, sniper presence, and mortars. Tracer bullets from machine gun fire went right through the trees. It looked like a steady red stream of light. The platoon hugged the ground to try to be under the incoming small arms and automatic weapons fire. The NVA began to "pop" their mortars inside the perimeter of the pinned down platoon. Shrapnel flew everywhere, grazing and hitting most of the platoon members. The situation was extremely grave. Ammunition was getting low. The company commander called for artillery support. However, the wrong location was conveyed to the artillery unit, and the initial blasts went the wrong direction. But the company commander did not have the time to correct the errant artillery rounds because the NVA was located in trees and bunkers on three sides of the platoon, and began shooting at will to the streambed, wounding the Company Commander. The Company Commander knew that reinforcements were needed as well as artillery and air support to fend off the overpowering force. He believed that if help did not arrive soon, this was going to be a massacre. The men fought for their lives. Morale quickly dropped. The medic was overtaxed, jumping from one to another to stop the bleeding. Snipers continued firing into the perimeter. It was difficult to move and more difficult to raise a weapon and return fire. In fact, little return fire came from the platoon as most sought some kind of cover from the oncoming barrages.

At 1111 hours the third platoon of Company B moved toward the contact site but was unable to progress toward the platoon duet to the intense fire being received by the second platoon. Instead, it was forced to remain at the top of the trail. It was able to place automatic weapons fire on the bunker complex, and able to fire at snipers. But the platoon was unable to reinforce Company B's platoon that was pinned down. At 1125 hours Company C began moving toward the 2nd platoon's location. At 1130 hours the first platoon of Company B also began moving towards them. Both platoons and Company C's objective was to surround the NVA positions in the bunker complex to cover the second platoon's withdrawal. At 1255 hours the first platoon joined the third platoon's location on the high ground opposite the hill where the fortified NVA positions were located. But both units were stopped because of mortar fire, this time heavily. The units were unable to proceed and could not cover the 2nd platoon's withdrawal. The 2nd platoon remained pinned-down for five hours.

The Battalion Commander believed the situation to be grave. The units on the ground under fire needed reinforcements to fight the NVA, surround the perimeter, and cover a withdrawal. The units already at the battle site were compromised and could not aid the 2nd platoon. Even Company C was not able to surround the perimeter as they too were hampered by snipers, mortars, and automatic weapons fire. Movement from the battle site would be difficult and a miracle as the NVA were determined to kill all the members of the 2nd platoon. Harassing fire and mortar rounds continually hit inside the perimeter. Snipers redirected their fire to place on the units on the hillside and keep them from rescuing the 2nd platoon. The battalion commander searched for answers. Artillery and airstrikes were directed on the bunker complex. He had hoped that this would hamper the efforts of the NVA and force them to stop firing on the pinned down platoon. However, this failed as well. In fact, the 2nd platoon received more intense fire after the rounds from artillery hit the bunker complex.

The battalion commander then decided to direct Company D, second platoon (about 21 men) to combat assault into the contact site. The landing zone was 400 meters uphill from the site. The platoon was met by the third platoon sergeant of Company B who gave the platoon leader, referred to as LTD as we learned from the "hump." The green paint of newness was worn off, and a more seasoned combat veteran was standing before the platoon sergeant. Quickly, LTD was given a situation report. The platoon began moving downward toward the streambed where the contact was occurring. At midway, the move encountered friendly artillery fire as it was mistaken for NVA movement due to the dense undergrowth in the area. Quickly, the radio operator communicated to them so that fire could be redirected. The unit responded and stopped the fire into the platoon. One man was injured from the falling shrapnel but was able to continue moving with the platoon. As they neared the contact site the NVA spotted them and placed small arms and automatic weapons fire on the encroaching unit LTD quickly responded and ordered most of his platoon to remain on the higher ground and place covering fire on the bunkers while he and several others maneuvered through the fire to assist in the removal of the wounded and direct the pinned platoon members to withdraw from the area.

"Ganes, Quick finger, Burk, Petey, come with me," said LTD.

"Quick finger set up machine gun over at that that tree and direct fire into the bunkers. Burk, Petey and Ganes fire into NVA positions, locate snipers," said LTD

The platoon leader LTD then moved to the contact site while the small element covered him. The platoon members look dazed and confused after all the pounding they had taken over the last six hours of intense fire. Ammunition was scarce, and many of the members did not have any ammo at all to shoot back at the enemy. A few of the platoon had secured a position in spider holes outside the perimeter and could not return to the rest of platoon due to heavy sniper fire. The Company D platoon leader crawled out to pull the persons from the spider hole, directed covering fire for the removal by getting the members of the 2nd platoon B Company to fire their weapons into the complex. LTD crawled 20 meters to the spider hole and talked the soldier into coming back to the perimeter. At first the soldier was afraid to move, but LTD became impatient and dragged him out under fire. His helmet was hit by a bullet while he was pulling him out. Once out he crawled with the soldier back to the perimeter. The covering fire by the small element was able to kill two snipers and destroy one bunker complex. LTD calmed the remainder of the platoon that was pinned down and ordered them to withdraw. He directed the upfront squad to continue covering fire for the withdrawal. He called Artillery and gunships on the bunker complex. However, at this point, unexpectedly, one of the bunker complexes fired automatic weapons again into the platoon. LTD took his small element and three members of the pinned down platoon with him and conducted an on-line assault against the bunker. As they were moving up the hill, the wounded Company B Commander ordered his troops to use what was left of the ammunition and cover the assault. Within 10 meters of the bunker, hand grenades were thrown, and the automatic weapons fire ceased. Three NVA soldiers put up their hands and surrendered. LTD brought the small element back to the perimeter along with the three captured soldiers.

However, the enemy countered with heavy mortar and automatic weapon's fire back into the pinned down platoon. LTD ordered more covering fire from the members of the second platoon, Company D on the higher ground. Covering fire also came from Company C and the two platoons of Company B. The troops all seemed to rally behind LTD and his small element. This appeared to work and reduced the machine gun and mortar fire. LTD again moved forward with his small element and directed the fire against the bunker. This time additional mortar and artillery support reached the top of the hill. Explosions were heard. Grenades again were thrown into the bunker. The machine gunners were silenced. This time there were no prisoners. The evacuations were again begun. LTD and his small element returned back to contact site and began directing the withdrawal. Sniper fire still continued to harass the troop withdrawal. LTD called for a napalm strike within 100 meters of their position along with F4 phantom jets dropping 300 lb. bombs. The impact was so loud from the bombs that many of the members of the platoons had blood coming from their ears and nose. It was devastating because some of the bombs landed within 30 meters of the location. But this time the unit had the upper hand, and the NVA began withdrawing. The withdrawal continued, still with some harassing fire. The final withdrawal occurred at 1700 hours the friendly elements commence withdrawing from the contact site. Airstrikes were employed to cover the withdrawal. The second platoon of Company D continued to provide fire support for the first and second platoon of Company B. Litters were made to evacuate the seriously wounded and the Company B Commander. The dead soldiers were wrapped in ponchos and also moved up the hill to the landing zone. Evacuation of the seriously wounded by helicopter was attempted but harassing fire and dense jungle prevented the removal. The litter bearers trudged 1000 meters up a 60-degree slope through a dense jungle in order to reach a suitable alternate landing zone to lift the wounded to safety. A stay-behind ambush was employed to block the NVA from following the Company's departure. A patrol base was set up. Company D platoon was moved back to their patrol base. Movement was heard throughout the night by Company B's listening posts as well as the radio relay team and Company A at LZ Delta. Results of the day's battle listed 35 NVA Soldiers killed in action. However, the US lost 2 men Killed in action (KIA) including the platoon leader of the 2$^{nd}$ platoon, Company B and 13 Wounded (WIA), including the Company B Commander.

*The Battle of the Streambed was finally over.*

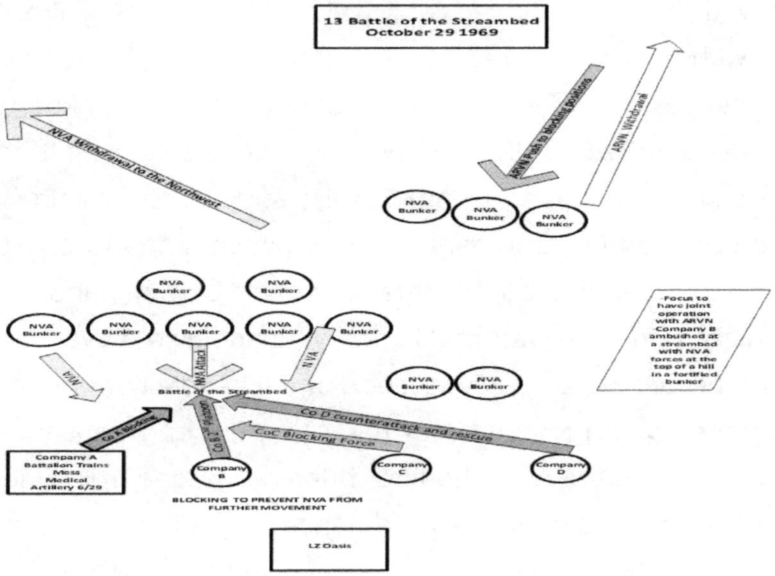


*Schematic Drawing 13—Battle of the Streambed*

# Mortar Attack

At 0625 hours October 30, 1969, a listening post from Company D began receiving small arms fire and B-40 rockets. Claymore mines had been cut during the night by unknown persons. Artillery was called to support the listening post to halt the impending ground attack.

As the artillery guns were being adjusted to assist Company D, LZ Delta began receiving a heavy mortar barrage from the East. The rounds were accurately directed on the fire direction center (FDC), the tactical operations center (TAC CP), and the mess tent. Troops from the artillery unit and the 4.2 mortar platoon braved the incoming fires to counter them. Numerous casualties occurred. Finally, at 0700 hours the enemy fire ceased, but not until 45 to 50 rounds of 82mm mortars impacted within the perimeter. Thirty-four US soldiers were wounded from the action.

The NVA moved toward Company C's location, after being stopped by the artillery strikes. An alert listening post observed them and began directing artillery fire on the moving soldiers on the trail. It was believed that a reinforced NVA company was setting up a bunker complex near the Company C's night location. At 1900 hours a flashlight was observed fifty meters from a listening post of Company C's. The men at the listening post watched as the NVA unit came within ten meters of their position. Claymore mines were blown which allowed the listening post to disengage from their location and return back to the patrol base. At 2230 hours the radio relay team also heard movement. This time the team received small arms fire and mortar rounds. The radio operators called for artillery and mortar support which halted the NVA attack. Still another movement was observed by a Company C listening post at 2320 hours. Artillery was employed again, halting movement. At 0202 hours the Company C listening post reported that its claymore wires were being cut. Small arms were fired; the remaining claymores were blown; and the listening post was called to return to the perimeter. Then at 0515 hours movement was again noticed by Company C. All the men in perimeter were put on 100% alert.

At 0635 hours the third platoon of Company D began receiving small arms and B-40 rocket fire. Mortars began exploding in the patrol base. Artillery and gunships were called to support the platoon. The hostile fire continued until 0650 hours, and then it stopped suddenly. Company A then left its patrol base to search for the withdrawing unit in the vicinity of Company D's contact. At 0732 hours Company A received eight to ten rounds of small arms fire. An hour passed and Company A again began receiving small arms fire.

At 0843 hours and again at 1050 hours Company A that was continuing its sweep of the area received small arms and automatic weapons fire from two directions. The company returned fire. Artillery and gunships were called in to direct fire on the suspected two locations. One NVA soldier was killed in action at the latter contact with numerous blood trails observed in the area.

*Figure 26 Using Dogs in Operations*

# *Halloween Hill*

At 1050 hours October 31, 1969, the point element of Company C moved down a well-traveled trail. A scout dog accompanied the unit to help them search for arms caches and NVA units.The dog smelled something on the trail and alerted the handler. A point unit was sent forward to investigate what the dog believed to be an unfriendly force. As it moved to the site discovered by the dog, an unknown-sized force-initiated contact causing immediate casualties. Realizing the gravity of the situation, the platoon leader reorganized his platoon and directed fire on the NVA's position, forcing them to withdraw. The platoon pursued the fleeing enemy but was forced to return to their night location in order to evacuate the wounded. Artillery was employed near the contact site. A Medevac helicopter was summoned, and immediately received B-40 rockets and small arms fire; but managed to pick up the wounded and leave the area to transport them back to a medical facility. A Second one was also called. This one was not as fortunate, as it tried to drop down a "Jungle Penetrator" (A sling for hauling wounded through the dense jungle growth.) to pick up the wounded. Small arms fire by the enemy sliced the penetrator, causing this operation to end. That penetrator was the last one available in the Central Highlands. The MedEvac was forced to return to base without picking up the injured soldier.

At 1223 hours new intelligence prompted a mission change. The Battalion Commander directed Company C to move North across the blue line toward their original patrol base. He also directed the Air Force to saturate the area around the blocking positions with air strikes. In accordance with the new mission Company C promptly began moving west. Artillery and gunships were expended in front of the moving column to provide cover and clear the area.

At 1227 hours Company C began receiving B-40 rockets from a NVA squad (8 men). The Company C Commander directed his company to establish a perimeter and wait for an artillery preparation in front of them. As the point element ascended to the halfway mark small arms fire began penetrating the lead platoon by an estimated platoon-sized enemy force (about 20 NVA). The Company Commander directed his two platoons online to assault the hill. His platoon leaders gallantly directed their men against the fortified bunkers. The NVA continued to intensify firing back at Company C. They also began sending Mortars into the perimeter spreading shrapnel among the line of soldiers as they moved toward them. The platoon continued to move to the top of hill. It now was in reach, and the Company Commander wanted to motivate his men to reach the top and neutralize the NVA unit by taking them out and overpowering their positions.

"Let's take the Hill." shouted the Company Commander

"Charge!" the men shouted in unison.

*Figure 27 Platoon on Maneuvers through the Jungle and Underbrush*

The platoons moved up the hill quickly, firing and maneuvering. The NVA countered. It was now estimated to be a reinforced NVA Company (about 100 NVA). The NVA now intensified their fire by aiming at the flanks and rear as well. In other words, the Company was receiving fire from all sides. The Company quickly formed a perimeter and returned fire. At 1512 hours after 69 minutes of combat, the Company Commander was wounded. Even so, he continued to direct the attack, and again became wounded. The two platoons continued their push toward the hilltop. One platoon leader disregarded his own personal safety by exposing himself to NVA fire to direct artillery rounds on the NVA positions. The platoons were within reach of the hill but were unable to move forward or rearward because of the intense fire. The Battalion Commander determine that the contact now has become a tactical emergency and immediately dispatched TAC AIR (Air Force F4 Phantom Jets) to the location to drop HE (high explosives), napalm (incendiary bombs), and bombs on the reinforced bunker complex. By this time, both platoons took a heavy toll of casualties. The platoon leaders continued to encourage and direct their men to hold their position and to still attempt to "Take the Hill."

The Battalion Commander flew above the contact site and to support the platoons by adjusting artillery strikes and directing gunships. He ordered Company A to move into Company C previous night location. The first platoon of Company D was then ordered into Company C patrol base on Hill 1240. The two platoons were able to withdraw at 1700 hours under the cover of a smoke screen. Tear Gas (CS) was also placed on the contact site. Artillery, gunships, and mortars were used on the NVA locations. The second platoon remained on the top of the hill to cover the first platoon and the Company's withdrawal. The Air Force F4's dropped 250 lb. and 500 lb. bombs throughout the contact area. "Moonglow" provided the light to assist the invincible "fire dragon" or "Spooky" which expended its deadly array of munitions throughout the night on the enemy locations. At 1800 hours sniper fire harassed LZ Delta. Also, later that evening LZ Delta's listening posts detected enemy movement outside their perimeter.

Engineers were repelled near Halloween Hill to construct a landing zone to evacuate the wounded. Sniper fire hampered some of this operation, but the engineers worked continuously into the next morning to construct a suitable landing zone. Two attempts to extract the wounded were made. The first was at 2130 hours with six of more seriously wounded to be evacuated. The second attempt was at 2300 hours. Each evacuation was marred by harassing fire directed toward the helicopters, but fortunately without any damage. The wounded soldiers were successfully removed. Results of the battle listed two US soldiers missing in action (MIA) and 22 soldiers wounded in action (WIA). The NVA losses were 76 killed in action.

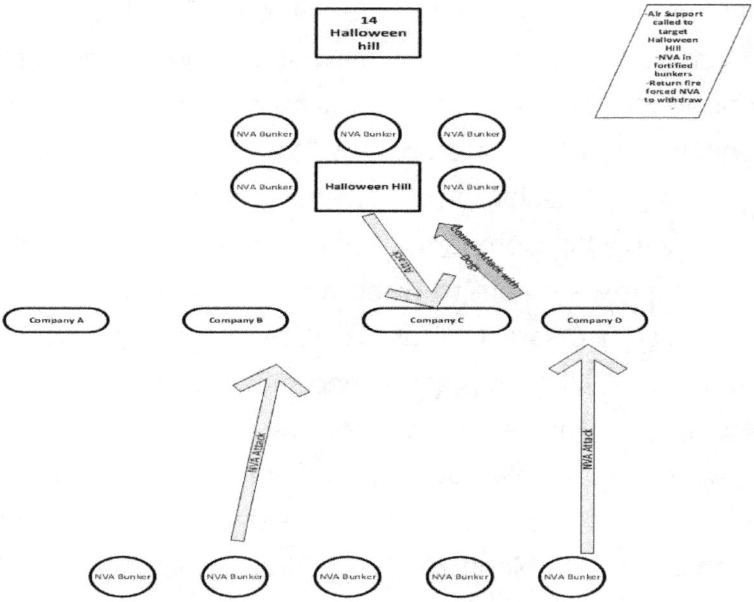


*Schematic Drawing 14—Halloween Hill*

Enemy movement was observed for the next three nights—November 1, 2, and 3. However, no contacts occurred in that time. On November 4th, the reconnaissance platoon found a 40-bunker complex with bunkers heavily fortified and built with "A" frame roofs. Five US weapons were left behind during Company C's withdrawal but were not found in the bunker complex. The weapons were still missing. The platoon found rucksacks which were searched for documents and weapons. One AK47 rifle was found as well as 25 Chicom grenades. A blood stained NVA shirt was also found. Other equipment was found in the complex such as mess utensils, food, rice, and medical supplies. Footprints and rice were also found in the area and on trails. Even the landing zone that was cut for the troops the previous day showed signs of NVA movement. Found were footprints and rice in the LZ. One US soldier was found dead, making Company C's casualties list to read 1 KIA, 1 MIA, and 22 WIA.

The next day on November 5 the NVA fired 24 mortar rounds, with 20 impacting within the perimeter of LZ Delta. For the second time in six days, the artillery and mortar men responded to the challenge by exposing themselves to the intense fire in order to counter it. At 0705 hours intense ground to air fire was received by gunships. More artillery was placed on the enemy positions. Finally, the hostile fire ceased.

With intelligence reports indicating that the enemy force was moving eastward, the battalion commander directed each company to move from their present patrol bases southeast to search for arms caches as well as for the NVA presence. For thirteen days the companies did not see any presence of NVA or arms caches. Sporadic sniper fire harassed some of the patrols, but the results were insignificant. On November 18 Company A found an arms cache through the help of a Kit Carson Scout. (Kit Carson Scout is former NVA soldiers that decided to help the US on the battlefront). No other contacts or arms caches were found. The NVA unit activity was becoming less in the Chu Pa Valley area and newer developments were starting to occur in the Plei Mrong area. Because of this latest information the battalion established a fire support base Gloria Ann and began Operation Hines on November 24.

# Plei Mrong—Operation Hines

The operation rendered the 631 NVA Regiment ineffective in the Chu Pa Valley area. The Battalion and its attached units suffered 7 US soldiers Killed in Action (KIA), four of which were battle related and three were non-battle deaths. There 72 soldiers wounded in action (WIA). On the other hand, the enemy lost 112 NVA killed in action and an unknown number of wounded.

The Battalion Commander of 3rd Battalion, 12th Infantry stated the following:

***"....The operation was a success....the joint US and ARVN fire base concept works well. The operation provided significant information on the 631st Battalion's re-supply route....the operation disrupted, temporarily, their (631 NVA Battalion) ability to move and resupply freely...."***

The Battalion was combat assaulted by helicopter into the Plei Mrong area. Sporadic contacts and finds of Viet Cong Booby Traps, VC training camps, NVA hide outs in caves, fortified bunker complexes, and NVA bodies along the trails indicated a strong presence of hostile activity in the area. No major contact occurred until December 7. On that day, the first platoon of Company D encountered a platoon-sized force (about 20 NVA). They were well-entrenched and located just outside their patrol base. Intense small arms fire and automatic weapons were directed on the platoon. One of the medics, a conscientious objector nicknamed "Doc," dealt with the wounded and continued to brave the fire. Wounded, "Doc" kept going until all of the wounded were addressed. When he finished attending the wounded, he went back to the rear of the perimeter to bring up ammunition to the machine gunner, who continued to fire non-stop into the NVA bunkers. "Doc" showed the type of courage and determination that the men in this unit continuously displayed against an NVA force.

# Christmas in Ban Me Thuot

The Battalion operations moved southward to Darlac Province in pursuit of Viet Cong who were in the area. There were few incidents during this period, just some sporadic sniper fire and a few mortar rounds placed toward company perimeters with light casualties. However, an experience occurred that is most unforgettable and spiritual in nature. Our unit secured a perimeter which included a stable in it. On December 23rd about 1000 hours while the platoon was holding a defensive position, there was a noise that sounded like light thunder. The sound grew stronger. No one had heard this type of sound before. It was not artillery; it was not mortar rounds; or it was not small arms fire or automatic weapons. Just off to the east of the perimeter gray shadows were seen emerging from the jungle. These were elephants. There were five elephants coming directly to our defensive positions. These were wild elephants, not tamed or not used for utility or cargo carrying. They stirred up the red dust that followed them. The elephants moved to within 25 meters of our positions and kept coming.

"Look Out and Take Cover," shouted LTD, the 2nd platoon leader of Company D.

The elephants ran over the defensive positions while the soldiers hugged the side of the holes they had dug. It was an unusual sight and unusual circumstance. The elephants continued going through the perimeter knocking down the mess facility and going over the next group of defensive positions. They kept on their run. They did not break their stride while going through us. After it was over, everyone laughed. It broke the tension of the snipers, the booby traps, the ambushes, the contacts, and the daily routines. This lasted only a few minutes but gave us a memory that could not be forgotten.

*Figure 28 Red Cross "Donut Dollies" Visit the Troops*

About 1330 hours, the platoons were surprised by an unexpected helicopter landing. It was a ***Red Cross helicopter.*** Aboard the helicopter were Red Cross Women who were fondly called "Donut Dollies." The helicopter brought donuts, some token Christmas gifts, and bearing good cheer to the perimeter. The girls set up a table near the helicopter and set out donuts and coffee for the troops in the perimeter. For those who were not on guard duty, they could come up and talk to the "girls" and get a donut and a cup of coffee. After being in the field for at least six months, women were an unusual sight. It was especially satisfying to see them bravely fly into a battle zone. This was, however, considered a safe area where few incidents were reported. But what is a safe area in a war zone? The "girls" were American and "round eye." After about an hour of entertaining the platoon members, the helicopter left with the

"Donut Dollies" aboard. We all wished them well on their next journey. It was certainly a morale booster.

That evening the battalion chaplain wanted to conduct a Christmas service. He had solicited assistance from the platoons to move bales of hay into the stable into rows resembling church pews. He moved a table into the stable as a pulpit. The service was to begin about 2300 hours so that it would pass midnight to celebrate Christmas day. The stars were especially brighter that night, with one star significantly brighter. The inside of the stable was lighter because of it. The chaplain only had to use one candle to see his sermon.

Because we had to maintain the perimeter defense, only a small fraction of the soldiers could come to the service. The chaplain began the service to remember those fallen soldiers in our previous contacts and began giving the sermon. After it was over, the chaplain proceeded to each defensive position to give grace to the soldiers manning them. This uplifted all of us that night and made an unforgettable experience in a place where the events often caused misery. Morale instantly improved and we were ready for anything else that may occur that night.

On Christmas day platoons resumed their patrols outside of the perimeter, the artillery strikes, and the listening post. There was movement detected the previous night, but no enemy soldiers were seen that day. Christmas Eve and Christmas Day were a day where no incidents occurred. We do not know if the enemy respected that day or whether strategically, they moved to another area. But we were thankful to get a reprieve. Operations continued to the end of the year without incident.

Ban Me Thuot was an area that was rumored to be a pivotal point for hunters to hunt tigers and elephants. It was the playground for Kings, Country Leaders, and wealthy entrepreneurs. The war in Vietnam reduced the number of hunters arriving to a minimum. The rumor was that President Teddy Roosevelt used the large hunting lodge as a base for some of his hunts. I can only imagine in those days that the journey to Vietnam would have to be by ocean liner rather than airplanes. The journey would have taken a few weeks to go over, time to stay for the hunt, and another few weeks to return. The hunting lodge was in disrepair but elegant and large. It was ranch style with a wall around it. No one occupied it this time. The local villagers maintained what they could of it. It was a part of the past history that Vietnam was known. The Viet Cong did not believe in anything, even preserving historical buildings. How this one survived is anyone's guess.

Tigers were a big problem in this area. The villagers reported seeing them regularly. They would stay away from the village, but on a few occasions, they would come in search of food. Once in a great while one of the villagers would get in the tiger's way and be dragged off. It was just a way of life. Elephants were also captured to be the "beast of burden" and used to carry supplies for the town and to do heavy construction work. They were difficult to teach, but when tamed did an enormous amount of work. Water was a problem to insure it was safe to drink. There were no sewage systems in the town.

During this period while engaged in Ban Me Thuot, South Vietnam's President Nguyen Van Thieu attached a battle streamer to the colors of the 500 men of the 23rd ARVN Division who stood rigidly at attention in the morning sun. No emotion showed, but the bright bit of red and yellow ribbon meant something personal and something they would not forget.

The 23rd ARVN fought with the 3rd Battalion 12th Infantry on a number of occasions. These were called joint operations and were successfully employed.

The members that President Thieu has recognized were the victors in the battle of Bu Prang-Duc Lap, Quang Duc Province, which had ended less than a month ago, 1969. The fight was a bitter struggle, and one which the US military believed was a test of the ARVN's ability to fight on their own. But they countered each NVA attack with ferocity. There were two NVA divisions against theirs. By the time, this campaign against the two divisions of NVA concluded, the 23rd Division had virtually destroyed two regiments and badly crippled other NVA units. The 23rd Division was credited with killing 1,838 NVA and capturing eight prisoners. Also captured were more than 150 individual and crew-served weapons as well as a large number of supplies. Duc Lap became a rallying cry for all ARVN troops and was proudly displayed on their tanks.

# Summary of Fall Campaign

The 3rd Battalion, 12th Infantry, 4th Infantry Division, nicknamed the "Braves", conducted eight offensive operations in the year 1969. Operation Wayne Grey (March 1 to April 18), and Operation Green Bullet (October 18 to November 24) were the most significant event of the year. In March 1969, the "Braves" entered a North Vietnamese Army stronghold in the Plei Trap Valley. This was an area that was composed of huge division bunker complexes, supply depots, and resupply roads. After the battles of LZ Swinger, Hill 800, and LZ Brace, the enemy was forced to withdraw from the area. Artillery, gunships, and frequent air strikes aided the infantry companies in eliminating the enemy threat.

After a light spring and summer campaign, the battalion entered the Chu Pa Valley near Plei Djereng and the Polei Kleng Special Forces Camp on October 18, 1969. The four-day battle of the Chu Pa Valley included the Battle of the Streambed, the Heavy Mortar Attack on LZ Delta, and the Battle of Halloween Hill. After the battles ended, the enemy was decimated and forced to withdraw from the area. The 3rd Battalion, 12th Infantry pursued the fleeting enemy and located a large arms cache. They continued the pursuit to Plei Mrong where significant finds of caches and bunkers were made. The year 1969, one of continuous combat operations, was a successful one. The "Braves" met enemy threats and forced the enemy to withdraw.

# Chapter Five—Campaign 1970

The Battalion was then moved back to Camp Enari in January 1970 to secure its perimeter, and replenish its troops, give them needed rest, and provide showers, hot meals, and a barracks to sleep. Of course, during these patrols were ongoing around the base camp. At the edge of Camp Enari was Signal Mountain, a large mountain about 3500 meters in height that overlooked the valley. Antennas were placed at the top to give a longer-range radio wave for the troops. A temporary radio station was placed in the camp to give news of the "world", and music for the troops.

On January 11, 1970, the news spread quickly that Camp Enari was part of the bases to be turned over to the ARVN (Army Republic of Viet Nam) and that the 4$^{th}$ Infantry Division 3d Brigade, of which the 3d Battalion, 12$^{th}$ Infantry was a part, was returning home. General Abrams made the announcement at MACV headquarters in Saigon. He stated that "None Better" soldiers of the brigade are included in the Phase III redeployment from South Viet Nam, which reduces the authorized ceiling by 50,000 as of April 15$^{th}$, 1970. The reduction in force (RIF) is beginning.

The 3d brigade had over 1300 consecutive days of combat without a rest or stand down and is expected to return to their duty station at Fort Lewis, Washington by mid-April and inactivated. Several units though will remain in the war zone and not travel back with the rest of the unit.

# Camp Enari Sapper Attack

*Figure 29 Camp Enari Entrance*

The war continued with patrols outside of Camp Enari, searching of NVA units and/or Viet Cong who still inhabited the area. On January 19th, 1970, an Indigenous person (Vietnamese) who was a "Shit Burner", was spotted observing some of the defensive positions along the perimeter. His job was considered a skilled position within the compound and was given clearance to come into the base camp to do his job without additional scrutiny. This day was different however, as the Vietnamese moved strangely about the compound. At four o'clock or 1600 hours, the Vietnamese left the base camp to return home.

That evening about 2200 hours, movement was spotted along the perimeter on three believed sappers who were looking at the best place to bring their satchels across the barbed wire and enter the base camp. The bunker placed fire on the movement but could not see any results. At 2245 hours the sappers found a bunker that was not alert. The sappers threw a rock at the bunker, and the sentry did not notice or hear it. They stealthily crossed the barbed wire to the bunker, crawled inside and slit the throats of the two sentries. They then moved to their target, a helicopter sitting outside the hanger area. They quickly placed explosives on the helicopter, and then at a safe distance, exploded it. The sound woke all in the base camp. The NVA sappers quickly moved to leave it. But an alert sentry at another bunker saw them and engaged them. The two sappers were killed. In the aftermath, the bodies of the two sentries were found. The helicopter was completely destroyed.

## Monkey Hill

On February 2nd, a patrol spotted what was believed to be a tunnel complex in what was referred to as Monkey Hill, due to so many monkeys inhabiting the trees. Sniper fire harassed the movement forward to deter the troops from going up the hill. There was a steep cliff on the side of the hill, preventing an all-around attack up the hill. As the patrol moved within 150 meters from the base of the hill, the NVA was waiting for them in ambush. The NVA fired into it, wounding one soldier. The patrol returned fire and silenced the NVA unit. When they investigated two NVA bodies were found along with one rifle and one rucksack with documents. The patrol moved onward up the hill. There was no more sniper fire or presence of NVA around.

The point element spotted an open tunnel ahead of them. When they investigated it, they found a tunnel cut into the side of a hill, hidden by a huge rock and vegetation. The patrol leader had three men investigate the inside of the tunnel. The length of it was about 150 feet and about 40 feet in height. A stream was running down the center. This way the NVA had water for cooking and washing right there with rooms constructed of bamboo on two layers. They estimated that this could contain upwards to 200 men. The NVA must have left hurriedly because pots of water were still heating, and fires were still burning inside the tunnel. Since it was in rock, the patrol leader could not destroy it, but only report what they found. It is now marked as a location for an NVA unit to preside.

## Banana Leaf Hill

About four days later, the 2nd platoon, Company D came across a small NVA unit that they found getting water from a stream. They did not hear the unit come upon them. Quickly the NVA returned fire and moved up a small hill that the unit referred to as Banana Leaf Hill. The 2nd platoon established a defensive position. The NVA that were originally spotted were a member of a platoon-sized force entrenched at the top of Banana Leaf Hill. There were about 8 fortified bunkers at the top of the hill. The larger hostile force then directed their fire into the perimeter of the platoon. It was very intense incoming fire utilizing B-40 rockets and automatic weapons. The platoon leader was able to call in artillery toward Banana Leaf Hill. The platoon began receiving mortars impacting within their perimeter. The platoon was able to return fire. The platoon leader reacted to the offensive and decided to send two of the squads forward, one to cover and the other to move and vice versa to engage them in a fight. The goal was to eliminate the automatic weapons fire coming from the bunkers, and if possible, to move the NVA off of the hill. The movement took about two hours to go from the base hill up about 250 meters until they were able to get within 20 meters of the first bunker. Automatic weapons fire was directed at them. The squad leader threw grenades into the bunker, as well as directed automatic weapons and small arms against it. The occupants of the bunker fought briefly and then abandoned the bunker. The squads did the same thing to the next bunker, with the same result Some of the NVA began to down the backside of the hill. The platoon leader had carefully placed a squad to function as a blocking force who engaged the fleeing NVA. Two of them surrendered and threw down their weapons. The others did manage to get away. When questioned, the prisoners were able to recount their story to the interrogators. One of the prisoners taken in this encounter was Phung Van Thinh. His story is as follows:

"Before being in the North Vietnamese Army, I was a student near Hanoi. I was drafted into the NVA three years ago. I was sent south to 'liberate the area from the Americans. I was led to believe 70% of the area and 80% of the population were controlled by the North Vietnamese."

His unit was understrength and that living conditions were bad. His unit could not obtain food from villagers due to the possibility of being disclosed. If you were wounded the higher-ranking officers would not aide, and often cast you aside to fend for yourself. But, to convert over to the South Vietnamese Army even under those adverse conditions was not going to happen. The reason for this is due to:

- Communist indoctrination which stated that they would face a prolonged period of "maltreatment" by the Americans if caught.
- Members of the unit who appeared to waver in their loyalty were assigned to a three-man team which was

to keep watch over each one in order to intimidate wavering comrades.

- To rally to the other side was to give up hope for a return to the north to see their families again.
- I did not know how to rally, where to go, or whom to talk."

All of these were bottled up in Thinh as he remained hungry, was "homesick," and was in constant hiding. Now, he got his chance to rally and surrender to the American unit. He received medical treatment and a hot meal. He proceeded the next day to lead the unit to a bunker complex.

## Kit Carson Scout

On February 7th, 1970, the 2nd platoon Company D, along with Phung Van Thinh, moved about three kilometers from their contact site. As they proceeded down the trail, Thinh quickly notified LTD to have the platoon set up a defensive perimeter, and that he, the platoon leader, and three others were to move ahead to what he believed was NVA bunker. The defensive position was to serve as a blocking force in the event the NVA unit fled from the small unit. The small unit spotted two NVA near a bunker about mid-way up the hill. The immediately laid down fire, forcing the NVA to seek cover. The small unit moved forward toward the bunker. A grenade launcher was pointed at the bunker as well as machine gun fire into it. Fire was returned. But the return fire abruptly ended. Thinh stated that he believed they had fled. They moved forward and found the bunker, but it was empty just as Thinh had stated. They found one AK-47 rifle, a blood trail, and documents. Thinh was right and became a strong advisor to the American unit. Some referred to Thinh as a "Hoi Chanh" or a turncoat to the NVA. The American Army called him a "Kit Carson Scout," and this was a forerunner of having former NVA or VC soldiers incorporated in the units as they are in the field. This was a successful implementation and Thinh was recognized for his participation. Thinh went on to help many units identify NVA strongholds and get an upper hand to defeat them in battle conditions.

## Move to Camp Radcliff

In March 1970, the 3d Brigade 12th Infantry was moved to Camp Radcliffe near An Khe. This was the start of the move of the battalion back to Fort Lewis Washington. Camp Enari had to begin being evacuated with the coming of the turnover of the base camp to ARVN in April. The mission of the unit was to search and clear Viet Cong positions from Highway 19, so that convoy movement can occur without harassment or ambush. Members of units who were short on time left were to be at Camp Radcliffe for a period of time until redeployment in April. Those of us who still had time to serve in country were redeployed to other units.

# KING COBRA

There was limited contact in March, with VC units quickly hitting each unit and then leaving the area. Pursuits against them had no progress. Patrols were on going. Each day they would go out and search and sometimes would be out in the field for two weeks before returning back to base camp. They established patrol bases with artillery units and bunkers so that they would come back to the patrol base and use it as a central location to do their maneuvers and searches. One day, on March 12th, the patrol returned back to the patrol base, only to find the soldiers who remained back to defend the patrol base all staring at the main TOC (Tactical Operations Center). There was a snake inside the bunker. Quickly the patrol leader sent two into the bunker, with machetes drawn and rifles ready to engage the snake. No one knew what kind of snake it was, but it most certainly was disrupting the operations. The two men were nicknamed "Viper" and "Cookie." Viper went in first and saw movement in the rear of the bunker. The snake had positioned himself behind a bench. The snake reared its head again, and Viper swiped at its head, but missed. Cookie yelled, "its behind you." Viper turned around and took another swipe but failed to hit the snake. But the snake struck, and this time hit the machete. He struck again missing Viper. The snake crawled to the back of the bunker. Cookie chased it, armed with a machete and flashlight. The snake again rose with its spoon-like head and struck at Cookie, just missing him. Viper now had the snake in its sights and as the snake rose, Viper hit its head several times. Finally, his last blow silenced the snake. When they went over to it, they discovered it was a Cobra Snake over ten feet in length! After it was over, both Viper and Cookie decided that it would have been best if they had not volunteered for this one. Even so, everyone applauded their gallant efforts, and the TOC resumed operations. It took the infantry to save the day.

## R&R (Rest and Recuperation)

It was now time for a break in the action. All of us were given an opportunity to see different countries and to spend a week away from the war action. The places to choose included Thailand, Japan, Hawaii, Malaysia, the Philippines, and Australia. I chose to go to Australia.

As we flew into Darwin, everything appeared Red. Red dirt, red mountains, and a great seaport. We moved from Darwin to Sydney where accommodations had been made for us. The Australians opened up their arms for us as it was quite a change from a combat zone.

Juliet is the hostess for the R&R Hospitality Service. She wrote:

*"I'm Juliet one of the R&R Hospitality Service hostesses, and I would like to tell you about hundreds of invitations from Australians extending hospitality to you, a U.S. serviceman.*

*First of all, if you would like to spend a few days in the country, accept one of the invitations to stay with an Australian family on their ranch. While you are there, you will be able to do a lot of horseback riding, work with sheep and cattle, and (in certain parts of the state) do some hunting and fishing.*

*However, if you would prefer to stay in and around the city, then let us arrange for you to enjoy a nice home-cooked meal and a relaxing evening with an Australian family in their home.*

*For those who are interested, we have information on golf, tennis, sailing, rowing, diving, swimming, surfing, fishing, fencing—and about any sporting activity or hobby in which you could be interested.*

*In addition, we hold a "Mixer" party every Tuesday and Friday evening from 6-8 o'clock. Do plan to attend this because we have invited two hundred young ladies from in and around Sydney to enjoy the evening with you.*

*The R&R Hospitality Desk is located in the lobby of the R&R center and the Hospitality Service is conducted by the Australian-American Association in conjunction with seven other organizations, there are hostesses on duty every day of the week, including Sunday, from 8 AM to 5 PM.*

*We are looking forward to meeting you, so do stop by and see us as soon as you arrive in Sydney."*

All of us enjoyed our R&R and were treated very well by the Australian hospitality group. It was a return to "normalcy." After a week we all returned back to the war action.

## Searching for VC with a Dog Team

On March 18th, the 2nd Platoon Company D went on maneuvers again outside of Camp Radcliffe. This time a dog and its team from the 64th Infantry Platoon Trackers accompanied the platoon. Because of the fleeting nature of the Viet Cong and the increased number of incidents with ambushes and hit and run attacks, it was believed that a dog and its handler would be able to locate positions for the platoon to find and engage.

Tracking itself is an old military tactic used throughout American military history. The combat tracker team consists of a team leader, a visual tracker, a Labrador Retriever, and a handler. Added also to this team is the Kit Carson Scout and another scout dog. This now has become an effective team for uncovering activity by the VC or NVA.

The new team and the 2nd platoon went maneuvers to locate a VC unit that was known in the area. About 15 kilometers northwest of An Khe, it was reported by an informer that the VC had encamped overnight. As they were moving on the trail the dog sniffed a footprint on the trail. The handler noted that it represented a place where a weapon was put down in a rested position. The team was now alerted to a presence of VC in the area. The dog and handler then sniffed at broken twigs, moved rocks, and imprints on the trail. The Labrador Retriever, known for its unique ability to track, keeping silent rather than having a bloodhound do the tracking. The Retriever also adapt well to the tropical climate. The scout dog on the other hand is present to provide early detection to prevent them from going into an ambush. Retrievers are too friendly and may lick the VC. The scout dog is more ferocious.

At 1015 hours a sniper bullet was fired above the heads of the unit. It came from the Northwest. There was only one bullet and seemed as if that was the only incident that was to occur. However, the scout dog sensed danger, and barked a warning. The retriever had sniffed evidence of a small unit that passed on the trail. Silently, after being warned by the scout dog, the platoon moved forward, one small unit at a time. They came across five VC sitting down to a meal of rice. They immediately opened fire, killing three VC. Two of them managed to escape.

When they came to the campsite, they were able to recover 3 AK-47 rifles, three Chi Com grenades (Chinese-made hand grenades), and a document that contained unit plans for the next month. Pursuit of the two VC that left did not bear fruit, this time. The result was a successful deployment of a canine team in its quest to locate the Viet Cong.

## *Irish Hill*

On March 23rd, the 3rd Platoon of Company B conducted a helicopter assault into LZ Ireland. Intelligence officers believed that a heavily armed NVA force was entrenched in a hill named Irish Hill. It was 850 meters high, with cliffs on the south side. At 0930 hours about 100 meters from the base of the hill, a member of the point element stepped on a land mine, blowing his leg off. The platoon had encountered a minefield, set up to protect a company-sized unit on the top of Irish Hill. Observation helicopters had noted about 40 bunkers on top of the hill, and also spotted an anti-aircraft weapon as well as heavy artillery. The platoon had stumbled on one of the main headquarters of the NVA (Believed to be a part of the 66th NVA Division). As soon as the mine exploded, the platoon began receiving mortar fire. The platoon leader called for an artillery strike on Irish Hill, as well as air power, both helicopter gunships and TAC AIR (F4 Phantom Jets). The platoon could move to aid the wounded soldier due to the location of the mines in the minefield. The rest of Company B was moved to the site, along with the combat engineering platoon to mark and remove the mines. Company B formed a perimeter and looked for an alternative way to move up Irish Hill against the large enemy force. One way was to climb up the cliff rocks. That would definitely surprise the NVA force at the top. The company command felt that artillery and air strikes would keep their heads down, where they would not notice the climbing troops. While the engineers were eliminating the mines, it served as a decoy as mortars were directed toward the location of the third platoon. The 1st platoon was ordered to remain with the 3rd platoon to bolster its defenses and to cover the engineer platoon as they defused the mines. The 2nd and 4th platoon were moved to the bottom of the cliff. The men used their climbing skills and ropes to move slowly to the top. One of them slipped and fell about mid-way up but was able to catch himself on a ledge about fifteen feet below where he fell. With catastrophe averted, the platoons moved upward.

At 1415 hours the first element of the platoons reached the top. The strategy was to attack each bunker with a grenade launcher, then a flame thrower, followed by small arms and automatic weapons fire. Each bunker was subsequently attacked using this method. One by one the platoons were able to eliminate the NVA in them, with many of them withdrawing from Irish Hill. At 1515 hours, the minefield was cleared, and the 1st and 3rd platoon began moving up Irish Hill. They did not know that the hill climbers had successfully completed the cliff climb and was attacking the bunkers. However, their progress was disrupted by sniper fire and several "spider holes" which were interspersed along the trail. The two platoons were able to close with the other two platoons at 1830 hours. There was no presence of NVA forces left at the top. A sweep of the area revealed fourteen NVA bodies, four AK-47 rifles, two 82 mm mortar tubes and munitions, and much evidence of drag marks and blood trails. They also found three NVA who were wounded and were captured as prisoners. The loss of lives for Company B amounted to one killed in action, and four wounded. It was quite an accomplishment under very trying conditions, especially the cliff climb. It was a bold move that made the battle more successful.

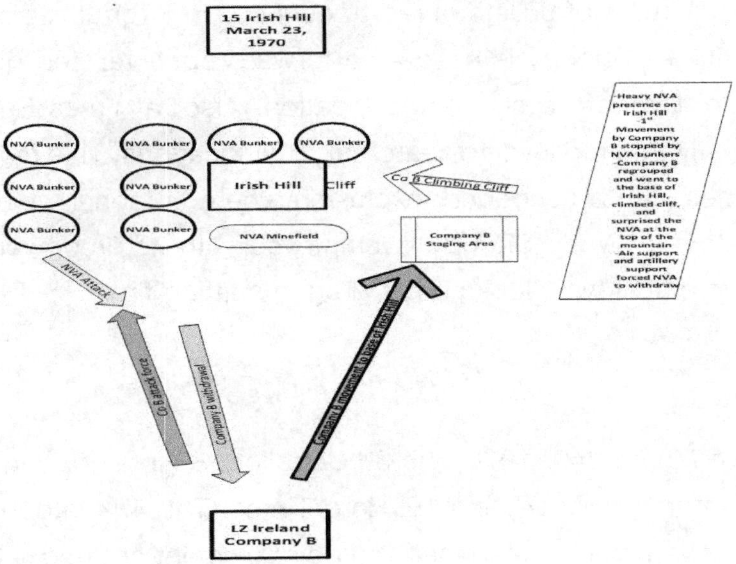


*Schematic Drawing 15—Irish Hill*

When questioned, the prisoners related that two companies of NVA were at the top of Irish Hill and that it was a headquarters for operations. They said their commanders were surprised at the cliff climbers in attacking their bunkers. They felt that the minefield would deter any movement up Irish Hill. They did not believe the engineer unit would remove the mines so quickly, and they further believed that the top of the hill would be able to be used repeatedly. They did not believe that they would be defeated in this battle.

To further pursue the fleeing NVA units that were leaving Irish Hill, "Snoopy was called in to place devastating fire around the vicinity of Irish Hill. Snoopy is an airborne personnel detector which sweeps over a suspected enemy location and looks for hostile forces. Many locations were found by this technique. Once found Snoopy places deadly .50 caliber machine gun fire on NVA and/or VC strongholds. It looks as if there is a steady stream of bullets of red tracers coming from the aircraft. Sometimes Snoopy is used as a forward observer and directs artillery fire onto a suspected location. Also, at times Snoopy would fly tree top level to search for NVA locations. This resulted at times with a secondary explosion where shrapnel would hit the aircraft. When Snoopy is employed with its firepower, the infantryman says it looks like a dragon spitting fire.

## LZ Hard Times

On March 24th, 1970, the 3rd Battalion, 8th Infantry engaged in an operation near LZ Hard Times. The 4th platoon was conducting maneuvers when the point element spotted a truck that was stuck in the mud alongside a little used road. It was near nightfall, and the unit was getting ready to select a night location. There was no sign of any NVA activity along the trail, and the sighting of a truck with Chinese markings was very suspicious. The platoon leader had a "feeling" about the truck. It just did not seem right. The platoon leader decided he wanted just to listen and see if there were odd sounds or movement. He sat with his platoon sergeant, and both began hearing the same thing. They did hear footsteps in the jungle, with twigs cracking. They also heard safeties clicking on rifles and rustling noises. It appeared as if the truck became disabled, and the NVA wanted to use it as a decoy for the US troops. They were on the move against the 4th platoon as they had observed their presence near them. Suddenly, the NVA started attacking their patrol base with mortar fire. They had stealthily surrounded the unit on three sides and opened fire with small arms and automatic weapons. However, the platoon leader, with his hunch about the truck being a correct one, rounded up his men who had not completed digging defensive positions, and regrouped to direct fire against them. Because they were surrounded on three sides, the platoon directed an online assault against the front element, surprising the NVA. They quickly overran their positions and started working on the left flank who was undermanned. The left flank quickly surrendered. The right flank disappeared into the jungle. The "hunch" paid off,

The platoon set up their night patrol base and was ordered to pursue the fleeing NVA the next morning. Artillery and air strikes were employed against the positions of the NVA as they fled. Results of the battle included 5 wounded US soldiers, and 4 NVA killed in action. One NVA was captured and removed back to headquarters for questioning. On the removal from the site, the NVA soldier was placed in the helicopter with me, who also was returning back to headquarters. It was an awkward moment for both of us. Each of us stared each other down during the journey, with each of us thinking we would push the other from the helicopter as we proceeded to headquarters. The trip lasted 25 minutes, but it felt like hours as it was uncomfortable. We arrived safely, and the prisoner was interrogated.

# Change of Camp Enari to ARVN, and Camp Radcliff Restoration

In the meantime, on April 15 under a ceremony attended by the top brass (high ranking officers) of the US and the 47th ARVN Regiment, Camp Enari changed command hands from the US to South Vietnam. The Vietnamese commander Lieutenant General Moang Lan and the US General Arthur Collins signed the agreement to make the move official. Both national anthems were played, and the flag of South Vietnam replaced the American flag. It was considered a momentous event and marked the end of four years that Camp Enari was a part of the 4th Division history. After the ceremony only a small number of US advisors were left in the camp.

The 3d Bn., 8th Infantry was moved back to Camp Radcliffe to support the engineer battalion who was remaking the base camp. They were charged with making a miracle happen in their reconstruction. They started the end of March and ended ten days later with the revamping completed. There were more than 750 men assigned to the engineer battalion, and all applied their many talents to the building project. The base was to be "custom tailored." The goal was to construct new bunkers and observation towers. Three Tactical Operations Centers (TOC) were also constructed. Additionally new rifle ranges, storage warehouses, and more than 200 two man fighting positions had to be placed within the base camp. The plans for the reconstruction were designed in August 1969 and the camp was to be three times larger than Camp Enari.

Tons of nails and thousands of board feet were trucked to Camp Radcliff from supply stations at Qui Nhon and Cam Ranh Bay. Additional combat engineers from the 299$^{th}$ engineer battalion and the 20$^{th}$ combat engineer battalion were transported to the base. The construction was done in two phases. The first involved the strengthening of the perimeter defenses by constructing Pepke bunkers named after the divisions former commander and dozens of new guard towers. The second phase was to rehabilitate the living and working areas for the division headquarters and its first and second brigades. Camp Radcliff was restored to a much better reinforced base. In fact, another new venture to restore the base to its previous days was called "bananamania," which was beautifying the base with banana trees. From this effort 95 banana trees were planted ranging from three feet in height to over ten feet.

# Cambodia Campaign

During April, intelligence reported that the NVA was making huge concrete bunker complexes in Cambodia just three miles from the border of South Vietnam. In and around the 16th of April a large cache of weapons was found near the Plei Djereng area. Munitions found were B-40 rockets, 82 mm mortars, AK-47 ammunition, C-4, Dynamite, Rifle Propelled Grenades (RPG), one anti-aircraft weapon, one .50 caliber machine gun, and three 60mm machine guns. Also found were a cache of AK-47 rifles still in wood cases with Chinese markings. The cache was found in a tunnel complex and hidden from view. The team now referred to as the tunnel rats found multiple tunnel complexes in the region, some fortified. Most were primitive though and just used for overnight or short stays. With information becoming prevalent in the 4th Division that the NVA was building their units in Cambodia, the Division commander looked at a new strategy that went beyond politicians. The politicians in Washington DC did not want to expand the war beyond the borders of South Vietnam. There were many restrictions on the operating units to not enter Cambodia. However, the situation became worse and the Division Commander, his intelligence officers, and his staff decided to make stand. At the end of April, the 3rd Battalion 8th Infantry was ordered to move the battalion by convoy to the Plei Djereng area and set up patrol bases in preparation for a future mission. The convoys were all loaded, but one thing was missing MAPS. No one in the convoy (Junior officers and enlisted men) knew where they were headed. The convoy moved out on April 29th to Plei Djereng from Camp Radcliff, an eight-hour journey. However, the journey took longer than expected and took about three hours more to arrive at the Plei Djereng air strip.

Patrol bases were set up and patrols were sent out to look for any NVA lurking in the shadows of the trees. No NVA were spotted. The next day rations and ammunition were issued to the troops. At 0600 hours on May 2, 1970, helicopters arrived at the air strip and began transporting troops into Cambodia. I was on the first helicopter to land at LZ First Born. The landing zone was expected to have heavy fire against the landing "choppers." But the LZ was cold, and the landings continued throughout the day. The battalion established a base camp as well as patrol bases to begin the operation. The 1st platoon, 3d battalion, 8th Infantry was the first to spot a fortified bunker at the top of a Ridge.

The platoon leader called for artillery strikes against the bunker. No return fire was received. The platoon slowly and carefully moved to the top of the Ridge to locate the bunker. Once they arrived it appeared as if all of the NVA had left the area. It certainly was well fortified and made with concrete and steel. It was camouflaged and difficult to see with netting covering the bunker. The platoon was ordered to explore it. Once inside it, the platoon could not believe its eyes. It had ten rooms constructed of bamboo, complete with hospital beds, an operating room table, a cupboard full of medical tools and instruments, a large mess (meal preparation area) and sophisticated cooking burners and utensils. A parapet was also found outside the bunker with 122 mm rockets, 82mm and 60mm mortars, cases of AK-47 shells, cases of Chi-Com grenades, RPG weapons in cases, four 250 lb. bombs that were fully loaded but not exploded when hit, and many other munitions. This was not the only bunker found with extensive weaponry and living quarters.

The battalion proceeded to destroy the bunkers. After about a three-week operation, the battalion was moved back to the Plei Djereng area to conduct operations. The Cambodia excursion was considered successful in that it uncovered huge bunker complexes and weaponry used against the village of Dak To. When the large caches were destroyed it took a large bite out of the NVA's supply of munitions and weapons.

## CHANGE IN STRATEGY- SUMMER 1970

Intelligence reports again were getting information that the NVA was rebuilding in Kontum province of which Plei Djereng was a part. During a period of increased combat activity in May 1970 it was believed that the NVA and VC suffered numerous casualties after they launched large scale operations –usually battalion-sized attacks- against the Fourth Division landing zones and fire support bases. But nearing June and the monsoon season, the tactics against the West and the US changed to that of VC-type terrorist activities. The new strategy was to employ hit and run strategies to harass villagers and troops in the field. Also, the tactic was to minimize the beneficial effects of the C-5 programs or civic action programs. Additionally, the VC and NVA focused on bridges and roads by placing mines as well as ambushes to hinder convoy and troop movement. Supplies were to be disrupted that were transported from Qui Nhon and Cam Ranh Bay. Highways 14 and 19 were often the targets as they connected to the major cities of Kontum, Pleiku, and An Khe. Also targeted were pump stations and gasoline pipelines along highway 19.

The 4th Infantry Division changed its tactics and assigned small unit operations to counter this strategy. This proved successful, especially in the incorporation of SRP's (Short-Range Reconnaissance Patrols) and LRRP (Long-Range Reconnaissance Patrols). Their role was to call in tactical air support to bomb the area with both napalms, HE (high explosives), and 250 lb. bombs. They also were successful in locating moving groups of NVA and VC by calling in artillery strikes on target to stop their infiltration. The use of SRP's and LRRP's took the pressure out of moving platoons on patrol, and instead focused on finding the NVA and VC with minimal contact needed. The patrols were still necessary but used the information more wisely. The monsoon rains which were the friend of the VC and NVA in the past were now used against them.

Because the focus was on Highway 19 and the potential ambushes along the route, a portion of the unit was moved to the seaport of Qui Nhon so that the division could set up a headquarters detachment. This enabled the unit to focus more closely on the small NVA and.

On June 12th, during this time as a platoon leader I was sent to An Khe to gather payroll checks for the troops and ride on Highway 19 on a ¾ ton truck. The trip to An Khe took six hours. However, along the way several incidents occurred. The truck was following a convoy which contained pumper trucks filled with oil. An NVA unit began firing 122 mm rockets into the convoy, which stopped it from moving forward. The NVA shot RPG's (Rifle Propelled Grenades) into the convoy. The drivers quickly got out of their tankers and began firing back at the NVA position. Our truck also stopped, and three of us in the truck also got out. The position was only about 100 meters from ours. I quickly called in artillery as well as gunships to stop the attack. Then, the three of us moved toward the position firing at will directly at their position. Soon we were receiving one automatic weapons fire and small arms against us. We kept moving toward them, and when we were within 20 meters of their position, began throwing grenades. After each explosion we continued toward them. When we got within five meters and shot into their position, NVA quickly withdrew. When we came back to the convoy, the drivers honked their horns, started their engines, and the convoy moved. We finally reached our patrol base destination and were able to hand out cash and payroll checks to our troops. The NVA could not stop us that day but proves the intelligence report was correct.

## Incident at a Bridge Security Point, the "Coke Girl"

In June, many small encounters occurred just like the one above. Small NVA forces or VC ambushed a convoy to interrupt supply movements. In another incident on June 26th, a bridge security was being visited by a local Coke girl who frequented the bridge patrol on a daily basis. Today when she arrived with her driver (She would always sit on the back of the motorcycle.) she was not smiling as she did normally to the troops. She offered her product "Coke" (Coca Cola) for fifty cents. The troops often complied and purchased the Coke from her. As soon as she left, the troops thought she nodded her head toward the riverbank. Soon after two men clad in black pajamas moved toward the bridge security each carrying satchels of explosives.

These were two sappers. Their purpose was to kill the security unit and then place dynamite on the bridge to destroy it. Also with them were two small units of NVA placed on either side of the bridge security. They were hidden in the heavy vegetation. When the sappers appeared, the two units on either side began firing small arms into the mechanized unit. The unit quickly responded and called in artillery and air support to thwart the attack. The sappers realized they could not breach the unit and put explosives on the bridge. They quickly disappeared, along with the small units on either side of the bridge security. The attack was prevented with the help of artillery and air support. The next day when the "Coke" girl returned, she was arrested and taken into custody. Although she was not a Viet Cong or a member of the NVA, she was aware of the attack, but was forced to not warn the Americans at the site or she would have been killed. It is the threat of intimidation that was the strength of the VC and NVA. People were afraid of their lives.

## Civic Action Rice Production

An example of the civic action program which is ongoing around An Khe is discussed below. In July and August of 1970 units of the 4th Division participating in the Civic Action programs developed a better rice crop for the Montagnard tribes in the Central Highlands.

The miracle rice was code-named IR-5, and it was planted in ten villages outside of An Khe. The result was a 300% increase in harvest production than what the tribes were experiencing.

The civic action platoon taught the Montagnard how to cultivate and develop the new rice to help them improve their food supplies. The tribes were not doing very well and were experiencing a poor rice crop. The new rice IR-5 can be grown all year, rather than only seasonal plantings in the wet season, when villagers have a constant water source.

Programs like this one were designed to help improve the lifestyle of the Montagnard tribes. As a result, the hope was that they would be more receptive the US and West. The Montagnard tribes were known not to support any side in the conflict.

July of 1970 had no large NVA contacts, but many small unit encounters with small units of NVA and VC. The villagers faced terrorist acts at night, and no one was safe from the NVA. Also, the US was still reducing its troop strength, so the units were not as full as they once were. I left the area in August 1970.

# Chapter Six-Platoon Leader's Story

Most of us came from non-military backgrounds, diverse educations, and diverse work experiences. Many were in the military from a draft, the later by a lottery method. There were a number "volunteered" to serve as well. There were deferments—education, marriage, and hardships. A few rushed to an early marriage to avoid serving. Failures in school meant the cancelling of the education deferment, so much effort was taken to continue to get good grades and stay in school. Yet for the majority a draft always loomed once a young man registered at the age of 18. The draft may have been a motivational factor to join one of the four services and avoid being placed in positions of danger, such as combat. But for those who were drafted, the choice of service and the type of branch to serve was predetermined without choice.

Very few of the draftees had fired a weapon, been introduced to artillery, exposed to living in the outdoors, were physically fit, or had the desire to enter. Basic training was used to change the draftee into becoming a soldier. The draftee and the ones that volunteered were placed in the same basic training camp to learn the military ways to become a soldier. This was a unique challenge and one that there was a "weeding out" process in each step the training program. Physical conditioning was a large part of the eight-week basic training class. Once the course was completed the soldiers were trained further in their MOS (Military Occupation Specialty) in advanced training. After the training was completed, the soldiers were reassigned either to a unit, a training facility of a combat unit in Vietnam. Other training undertaken included parachute training, ranger tactics, jungle training, and escape and evasion. Once the training was completed, the citizen was changed into a soldier. It is a transformation as a result of a refined process.

My story is a little different. I was a college student at a community college studying business administration. I was not an outdoorsman or a hunter, and instead enjoyed reading books, playing golf, water skiing, snow skiing and watching basketball and football games. I was ordinary and smallish in stature. But some referred to me as a "daredevil" and one that took some chances and enjoyed the thrill of the challenge. While at the community college I was introduced to a ROTC (Reserve Officer Training Corp) two-year program that when graduated I would become a commissioned officer (rank of 2$^{nd}$ Lieutenant) in the US Army. My obligation was to serve 2 years in the active army and 4 years in the reserves with options to extend my obligation. I was scheduled for two summer camps between my sophomore and junior year and between the Junior and senior year. In the middle of my sophomore year, I transferred to the main campus of a Big 10 University to continue my education and be a part of the ROTC curriculum.

My college years were full of study, parties, library time, class time, attending ROTC training and drills, and preparing for the military. Colleagues of mine who did not feel they would be drafted were busy taking interviews with companies. Since I knew what I was going to do, interviews were on the back burner.

There also were students who were called "Greenbaggers." This group was anti-Vietnam and protested the war. The number protesting increased over the time I was at the college. One day I was walking to class and had my ROTC uniform on, one of the protestors and then several more started throwing tomatoes at me, stating I am a pig for supporting the war. The crowd got closer, and one of them threw me to the ground pelting me with more tomatoes. One person started throwing his fist at me and kicking me while I was down. There were too many to resist. This went on for about ten minutes, and finally one of the leaders said, "That was enough—our point is taken." They left, laughing as they left. I was sore, but really was not hurt. I went back to my room, cleaned myself and the uniform, and proceeded back to class. The protestors were located in another area of the campus, so there were no other incidents that day. I was told later that the movement was supposed to be non-violent, and that the protestors were comprised of non-students and professional protestors. However, no one knew for sure.

What I did not understand is that the war effort was by the authorization of the President, not of Congress. It was a "police action" and not a war. Congress did not approve of the war, but budgeted appropriations for the troops and equipment. The Army was executing the order by training and sending troops to Vietnam.

Another incident that I remember was me meeting the leader of the protestors. He identified himself as an Army veteran returning from the war. We discussed the political aspect of the war, and he stated that I was on the wrong side because my views supported military action, and his of course did not. He threatened me and told me to watch out for other protestors. I told him he was crazy, and that if he protested that is his right. But when violence starts, all bets are off. Protests continued until I graduated to begin my service.

After my commission, I was given orders to begin officer training. Everything seemed all right before I received the orders. Once received, it was somber occasion. It was the unknown going to a country that little was known, the language so different, and the customs much different than ours.

I began studying the country and the people, the religions, the government, the army and navy, and air capabilities. I learned Vietnamese language to better understand what is being said. I studied tactics and strategies to prepare for the war. After training I was assigned to be an officer of a basic training unit. This was also the first training received by raw recruits. There were all types of people from all backgrounds, education levels, language levels, creed, and color of skin. There were Indians, Negroes, Hawaiians, Mexican Americans or Latinos, persons from incarceration, and young men ordered to serve by a judge. Some were drafted, some were not. The first order of business was to teach marching in step to move from one location to another. Another step was to train them in physical training exercises. Drill Sergeants, most of which just returned from the war, began directing and shouting instructions. Classroom instruction was given by me and other officers of the training battalion. Range training taught them how to shoot, and the drill sergeants were diligent in training them. First aid especially battles first aid, tactics, strategies, and developing a unit and discipline were emphasized. I was able to go through three cycles of basic training for troops as a basic training officer. I received orders to begin my journey to Vietnam and was assigned to the 4th Infantry Division, 3d Battalion, and 12th Infantry.

First, I was to undergo Jungle warfare training in Panama to learn how to live in the jungle, how to survive, and to undergo more rigorous training exercises. The sequence of all these events gave confidence to new officers when they go to their units. Leadership training, tactics, strategies, living in the jungle, and enemy knowledge were taught to incoming troops. My feet though took a toll. For most of my time in Panama, my feet were in four inches of water. Jungle rot was common and set in. We would sleep on hammocks at night above the water. You could hear monkeys laughing as they watched us. Snakes were just a part of the journey and swam often in the waters we stood in. Even the rivers were different as the width of the river or stream was the depth of the river or stream. That meant from the bank it was straight down, and we treaded water across the stream. We often used zip lines to cross rivers if they were too large. We learned how to construct bridges and survive in a harsh environment. Once in a while we would see natives armed with hunting rifles as we were doing our maneuvers. One time while they were shooting at game the bullets came remarkably close to our location. It was a taste for what is to come.

The training ended, with a successful graduation as a jungle expert. Off to Oakland, California, and the plane to Vietnam. The flight was on a converted Flying Tiger cargo plane. The seats were mesh, and not comfortable. The first leg of the flight was to Anchorage Alaska. The next stage was to go to Ho Chi Minh City (now Ho Chi Minh City). The total flight time including layovers was 32 hours. We arrived in the early morning hours. We could see flare lights outside the plane window, with the rest of the countryside completely dark. There were no lights in the villages, or even lights in the cities. It was an eerie moment. There was an immediate sense of fear of a bullet or anti-aircraft round would hit our plane. Our plane turned off the landing lights and was unmarked going to the air base. We circled the airstrip until daylight and landed about 0530. We gathered our gear and walked off the plane.

Seasoned troops, having spent their time in Vietnam in combat and support units were waiting on the runway. They were dressed in new clothing to go back home to the "World." Some were on crutches, and their young faces now aged from all of the events they encountered during that year. Some were National Guard troops, some were Army, some were Navy, and some were Air Force and Marines. All had a common goal—leave the country now. As soon as we cleared the plane, the troops going home gave a cheer, said good luck to us (they referred to us as greenhorns or newbies), and hurriedly got on the plane, in the event of unexpected incoming. The plane took off quickly, and we all waved them off. Our turn was next.

We were herded off the runway into a waiting area, and bussed to the air base, where we sequestered in barracks and Quonset huts, refreshing ourselves and waiting for our unit assignment. Uniforms were issued, jungle boots, weapons given and assigned, field gear including canteens and compass, were given out. While I was walking down the street, I said hello to an older Vietnamese maid. She had black teeth (I found out it was a sign of beauty) and started yelling at me in a tone I did not expect.

Our movement to our unit was the next day in a Caribou C130. I was assigned to the 3$^{rd}$ Battalion, 12$^{th}$ Infantry located at Camp Enari outside of Pleiku. I had no idea where that was or what kind of terrain the base camp was located. The plane took off about 0800 to fly to Pleiku Air Base. The flight was expected to last about two hours. The Caribou had a back gate that slanted downward to accommodate paratroopers and load tanks and trucks into the cargo bay. This time the Caribou had strappings for seats, much like the aircraft had during the transport from the US to Vietnam. About forty minutes into the flight, a 50 caliber round went through the floorboard, narrowly missing me and going through the ceiling of the aircraft. The pilots moved the plane higher to avoid further rounds entering the plane. No other rounds hit the aircraft after that. The pilots stated that this was normal in their flights to the central highlands where Pleiku was located. As we neared Pleiku we could see mountainous terrain with triple canopy jungle covering them. It looked like an Appalachian Mountain range. Fog surrounded the valleys and clouds surrounded the mountains. The mountains ranged from about 500 meters to 2900 meters in height, according to the local sources. It seemed about right. We passed over a major highway, which turned out to be Highway 19 and saw the Mang Yang pass which was the location of where the French were defeated in 1954, which resulted in the French leaving the country. We flew into the airbase and were quickly moved by bus to the base camp. At the base camp we were orientated as to what to expect, assigned a company and platoon, and had a chance for a warm shower and a bunk bed. Hot meals were served. All incoming personnel were given three days of training on maneuvers outside the base camp. On one of the walks, a Montagnard fired a cross bow near our group, with the arrow going into the tree. As we continued the walk, trip strings were strewn on the trail, hiding a spear. If they had been tripped, the spear would have wounded or maimed the unlucky soldier. The training made us all aware that this was not a conventional war, and that it was an extremely dangerous country. No tigers, elephants, snakes, or other wildlife outside of some hogs and chickens were on the trails during this time. We even saw hooches, which were straw huts, some on stilts and others on the ground that housed the locals and harbored what we believed were Viet Cong at night.

The three days were completed, and the helicopters picked us up to fly to company's location. The Landing zone (LZ) was small in between tall trees. The helicopter was about ten meters from the ground and forced us to jump out of it as the terrain was very uneven making a landing extremely dangerous. We moved quickly off the landing pad and the helicopter moved on. Our initial supplies were dropped as well. Food was in the form of "C" rations. I was told to have enough to support two weeks of a "hump." The platoon was to search the ridgelines for signs of enemy locations and clear the area. The company commander was gruff, and short to the point. He weighed about 240 lbs. and was about 6'3" tall. He briefly told me what he expected his platoon leaders to do and introduced me to the outgoing platoon leader.

The outgoing platoon leader had finished his tour and was looking forward to returning back to his home, or as he referred to it as "the World." All of them called it the "World." I met the members of the platoon. There were seventeen of them in the field. Three had been removed due to disease and injury from the operation. There had been no contact in the last twenty days. Each platoon member had a nickname. The platoon leader was referred to as LT. Names were not important, and no rank was ever displayed on the uniform while in the field. On radio frequency, the platoon leader is the number of his platoon, and the company commander is 6. Higher is referred to as the higher-ranking officers. The outgoing platoon leader briefed me on the operations and spent the night underneath a poncho strung between two trees with a jungle blanket covering each man. A watch was put in place with a change coming every two hours. It was the platoon leader's responsibility to oversee the change of guard. The outgoing platoon leader then left on the early morning helicopter that dropped supplies off to the company. He wished us good luck and success on the future. The platoon now was mine alone to lead.

For the next 60 days, the ridgelines were combed and investigated and searched for the enemy. There was sporadic fire that missed us but had us knowing the Viet Cong were present and watching us. Mortars would hit our perimeter every so often. Our perimeter at night was often probed by rocks thrown to see if the watch was awake and not asleep. Our rotation system worked and our platoon members the next day were refreshed to have another day of search. Each of us had a ruck sack that contained our provisions, our jungle blanked, our poncho, extra socks, and a change of clothes. The ruck sack when filled weighed about 80lbs. I weighed about 140 lbs. So, it was very heavy on most days. On one of the searches, I tripped and fell. The steepness of the terrain and the heaviness of the ruck sack had me roll down the hill about 400 feet. It was a light moment for the platoon, as they all laughed to watch their platoon leader fall down the hill. I got up red faced and got ready for the next move up the next hill. Often, we had to go single file in the dense jungle, as there was not enough room to go side by side. A point man was always appointed for the day. It was a rotating position, although a few wanted to do point each day. I was the platoon leader and felt I would go number

2. The Viet Cong would fire at the point man, and then leave. A good point man would know where the enemy is, to avoid this from happening. At night we would send a small unit to set up an ambush area, lined with claymore mines. It was a way to listen for any enemy movement. Some call this a listening post. Their purpose was not to engage the enemy but to warn us if they are present.

Our platoon sergeant was twenty and had joined the Army after two years of college. Most of the platoon was 18 and 19. All of them listened and reacted without question. There were no discussions of politics or whether we should be there or not. All conversations were about the world. They wanted to know about it and what is happening back there. Letters were given from home about every two weeks with mail call. A few received packages from home with food, which was shared with all. With all the fog and harsh weather clothing was not exchanged very often, so that the men could not change clothes for the entire time of the operation. Two to three months is a long time to go with the same set of clothing. At times, food became scarce, which forced us to find food in the jungle, even eating bark off trees. Water placed in the canteens from streams required water purification tablets to go along with it. Any time the unit stopped; a perimeter was formed for protection. Maps were provided the platoon leader, and the company commander directed where the platoon was to set up and go. Reading a map was critical in the jungle. Helicopters regularly picked up troops to take to the next ridgeline during the operation.

Combat was an entirely distinct set of circumstances confronting the platoon leader, the squad leaders, and the platoon. At the first sign of the enemy or the first shot by the enemy, the platoon set up in a defensive position, formed a strategy, and moved toward the enemy fire. Mortars and artillery were called in to disrupt the enemy forces. We would move in stages toward the enemy focusing on automatic weapon positions and snipers. Our goal was to remove one at a time the enemy fire. When it became too intense a fight, an order would be given to withdraw, reorganize and attack again. All the men responded quickly and decisively. The injured were given first aid as quickly as possible. No man was to be left behind. When a member was missing in action, all efforts to find the soldier were done. A complete investigation was also conducted if the person could not be found. It is quite easy to be separated in combat if you are a part of the listening post or on ambush patrols away from the perimeter. Fortunately, there were few missing soldiers in action. He details of the missing in action are documented in the battle action reports in this manual. However, the consequence of becoming a prisoner of war (POW) was very real. That was the reason much effort was taken to eliminate those possibilities.

There are three more developments worth mentioning that the platoon leader oversaw in this tour of duty. The first was the recognition of the radio telephone operator. The second was the platoon medic. The third was the recognition that dogs played with their attendant in some of the maneuvers.

The radio telephone operator (RTO was responsible for all communication from the platoon leader to the battalion. This communication included combat action information and the call in of fire from artillery, gunships, war planes, and battalion mortars. Also, the RTO would call in Medevac's. The

RTO would be close to the platoon leader in all situations, so communications would not be lost.

The platoon medic, if you were fortunate to have one, helped calm the injured during battle conditions, and apply first aid to stop the bleeding and await transport to a medical facility. Oftentimes their actions saved the lives of the men that were wounded in battle conditions. Weather was often a reason a medevac helicopter could not land. Also, enemy fire would disrupt landing operations. Jungle harnesses were used to thread the trees to the injured and haul him back into the helicopter. Each medevac was done in extremely dangerous situations. The platoon would place covering fire to keep the enemy from firing toward the evacuation. Most of the time this technique worked and the injured were able to be transported from the field to a medical facility and be treated. The dead soldiers would also be transported by other helicopters. The bodies would be placed in a body bag and sent back to the quartermaster to be processed and sent back to their "home."

The third is the use of dogs to help search for enemy caches and positions. The dogs were assigned to a unit and would go everywhere the unit would go. They would be in point element and were trained to detect mines, booby traps, enemy soldiers lurking near them, and be the eyes and ears to help guide the platoon. There were many stories of heroism with the dogs and their handlers in battle conditions.

# Montagnard and Villagers

What does a Montagnard village look like? Montagnard are like our Native Americans and live-in isolated villages. Their huts are usually on stilts with openings on the bottom for chickens, food, and supply storage. The huts are usually in a circular formation, although some line the street that passes through their town. The men are usually the hunters that provide food, and the women are housekeepers. There are schools for the children, but they are home schooled by the "elders." The Montagnard hunt with cross bows that are made of primitive materials, with bamboo arrows. Sometimes the arrows are tipped with poison to kill or injure prey more quickly. Tigers pose a threat at night to these villagers, and in the last year over four persons were dragged away by a tiger searching for prey. The Montagnard are a proud people, and the men in their village were recruited by the Viet Cong to supply information, be trail guides, and play havoc on American forces by the setup of booby traps—spear traps, tiger traps, tree spikes, and pungi sticks. There is one chieftain in the village, an elderly man to whom the village looks up.

Most of the other villagers that are not Montagnard live in small clusters of huts. Their main purpose is to harvest rice and work the fields. They also raise hogs and chickens, and vegetable gardens. They are self-sustained. These villagers also were plundered by the Viet Cong at night, with the men taken from the village. Often, there were only women and boys under fourteen in the village. Fear always was present when the US troops entered the village, thinking it would attract the Viet Cong and that the villagers would be harmed by a crossfire.

The average income was a reported less than $100 per year per family, so there was not much buying power. Our interest in the villagers was to gain intelligence about the Viet Cong of if the North Vietnamese Army had passed near or through their location. The NVA would get food and supplies from these villages. There were many stories of rape, theft, and destruction when the NVA came through. The US soldiers were more disciplined, and those events did not seem to happen.

## Money and Transactions

Money exchange was another interesting thing. US soldiers had what is called MPC or Military Payment Certificates to use as money. US Dollars were not used. Only Vietnamese currency could be used in the villages to purchase local items. The MPC could be used to purchase at the Post Exchange or Commissary when a stand down occurred at the base camps. Most of the soldiers placed their money in a savings account established by the Army to have when they return back to the US after their tour. Of course, since the periods between stand down periods would be from two to three months, coke girls would come to the troops to sell coke products from a motorcycle. Sometimes the girls would be on the back with their partner in the front driving the motorcycle. A cold coke in 120-degree weather was welcomed by the troops. Coke girls were not considered a security risk. Periodically, the resupply helicopter would drop soft drinks and beer as well as SP (Sundry) Packs for the troops. However, with fog enveloping many landing zones, and monsoon rains, resupply helicopters could not fly. The same things occurred with clothing. There might be a month or more passing between changes of clothes due to the same weather conditions.

## Search and Clear Operations

The operation on searching and clearing on the ridgelines ended after three months. The company was brought back to Camp Enari to replenish its ranks, get hot food and water, hot showers, a bed to sleep in, and new clothing and shoes, if needed, for the next operation. For about two weeks, the platoon members enjoyed their hot meals. Now another test began. The company was moved by convoy to a landing zone and transported to the Plei Trap Valley. This was an area that was believed to be a NVA stronghold as it bordered Cambodia and Laos. There were many signs of infiltration routes in this area.

The operation details are listed in the 1969 operations. From a platoon leader's standpoint, the platoon sergeant and the squad leaders become an important asset in combat operations. The point men are selected due to their experience in detecting enemy presence. Dogs were sometimes used to help identify potential enemy areas. The dense jungle growth forced the platoons to go in a single file along an overgrown trail. Machetes were used to blaze a trail. At each step of the mission, danger lurked behind every tree growth, ranging from snipers to enemy observers watching our every move. In the early morning hours, or dusk hours at night, we could expect mortar fire or small arms fire to get near our perimeter. Each man reduced the weight of his ruck sack by trading or just eating fruit at lunch. C4 explosives were used to clear trees for a landing zone or dust off, as well as cook hot meals. The RTO was a key member of the platoon to keep the Command group in communication with our activities. Ambush patrols or listening posts were sent out each night to detect enemy movement earlier. These were not to engage, but observe, blow the claymores when approached, and get back to the perimeter if a fight ensued.

The platoon often returned back to the company perimeter at nightfall but was prepared to spend several days or weeks on patrol. Each night on the patrol base, holes were dug for protection against enemy fire. There were no sandbags available to construct a bunker, and holes had to be deep enough to protect. Map reading accuracy was a necessity, although with the terrain being fairly similar on a topography map, mistakes in location were often made. When that occurred, friendly artillery fire may be aimed at their location, oftentimes causing casualties. It was often said that the most dangerous thing in the Army was a second lieutenant with a map and a compass. However, it was not only the second lieutenant. Many others experienced the same thing. GPS was not invented yet. Very rarely was there a night operation with night goggles. Instead, the operations started at EENT (Early evening nighttime) or EDNT (Early Day nighttime) which is the time at night when the sun set but it is still light enough to see. The early dawn is when first light appears, until the sun rises above the horizon. Before those times it was dangerous to move in the jungle areas. There was an abundance of wildlife roaming the jungles at night up to and including Tigers and large snakes. Monkeys continually had motion in the trees, often mistaken for enemy movement. Orangutans were also spotted in the trees. On several occasions, these animals threw coconuts at our locations. King Cobras and types of cobra snakes covered many of the trails, creating hazards. The most dangerous snake of all was the bamboo viper, which was about 2 feet long and green. It was hard to spot, and when it bit you, the poison was so severe it affected the nerves of the body to shut it down. Jungle rats, at times larger than house cats, also roamed the perimeters at night foraging for food.

Ponchos were strung between trees to ward off rain at night and keep the soldier dry. The soldier covered with a jungle blanket to keep warm when sleeping. Soldiers rotated every two hours to keep an active watch in the event an enemy soldier was lurking about the perimeter. Often rocks were thrown to probe areas of the perimeter. If no response by the sentry, the enemy would probe further. Sappers would then set up their long stick of explosives and breach the perimeter.

There was always anxiety during operations and movement, perimeter set up and defense, and during landing zone arrivals and departures. It was always a relief to have a landing zone where there was no action. This was called the Cold LZ. If the helicopter landed among enemy fire, it was called a Hot LZ. For us, the number of Hot LZ's was few in number. Most were cold.

The morale of the troops was especially gratifying, as each one supported the other. They respected the orders given but were not afraid to speak up if there was a better way to do things. The platoon leader listened to his leaders and platoon sergeant. It was a way of survival in the jungle.

The company and platoon in Combat operations give you a perspective of war and the types of events that engage in the battlefield. The men who served were everyday heroes that serve as role models. All of them earned the gray feather. Some earned the higher colors, and all served honorably.

# Chapter Seven—Going Home

To the average soldier there were only two ways to go "home." The first was being wounded or killed, and the second to complete the duty assignment. There were others, of course, such as military justice convictions, unsuitable for the Army discharges, and hardship such as a family death or other event. The countdown mode was always being done in some way by all of us. Calendar dates were crossed off with the number of days left displayed. Weeks went by with all of us wanting another to pile on it as soon as possible. A year is a long time in combat.

We all wanted to be like the first group we saw, waiting on the "Big Bird" home. It did not matter what kind of airplane it was, just one that could fly way away from here. But how do you put this year aside and forget? Personalities have changed. Most of us grew far older than our years. Some had battle trauma, or as it was referred to as battle fatigue. We all had memories of those who served with us. Some went home in body bags, which were in some cases ponchos placed inside a body bag. Some of the wounded were airlifted to a Navy Medical ship or to Japan to recover. Others were sent to Germany, then the US. But all when recovered were sent back "Home."

When it was time to go back to the "World," the returning soldier would be picked up by a supply helicopter to the nearest air base, then flown to Bien Hoa air base for return to the United States by a contracted carrier. Normally, the troops were transported by a C130, or caribou to the air base. Upon arrival, they were immediately assigned a bed, a shower, and issued new clothes and shoes for transport in the next day or so back to the states.

I can remember my going 'home." I was in the process of being transported with a convoy back to the airbase to catch a Caribou to fly to Ho Chi Minh City and catch the next plane "home." Our convoy was ambushed and hit with 82mm Mortars and rocket propelled grenades. One truck was demolished, but most of them got through. I was one of the lucky ones. I was just 3 hours from my flight back to Ho Chi Minh City when the last combat action occurred. The Caribou was a very welcome sight. Those of us who were going on the flight back the states hurriedly got on the plane and waited anxiously to leave. But the Viet Cong had a different idea. The plane was riddled with 50 caliber rounds, but none of them damaged the motors or propellers. One of the wings had a hole in it, but it was still able to fly. The plane took off. Another 50-caliber machine gun round went through the floorboard. Again, there was no casualties.

We finally reached the airport in Ho Chi Minh City and were given clean clothes and new boots to fly home. All soldiers going home, regardless of rank, were assembled in a "Ready Area." A glimpse of the incoming passenger plane was spotted by one of the men. Cheers were loud and sustaining as it seemed almost impossible to believe that this day was actually here. The excitement grew louder as the plane neared the airfield. The "World" was becoming nearer and a reality to them.

When the plane landed, new troops in fresh uniforms embarked, and were assembled along with their gear, in a holding area. The drill sergeants would bark orders to begin moving them from tarmac into the terminal for further disposition into the country. There they would get their orders and their new assignments, as well as their scheduled departure. They passed us and all stared, wondering what they were up against.

It was time to embark. The men walked in a fast pace in a single file and boarded the plane. Once it was up in the air and headed for Tokyo, Japan for the first leg of the journey; the noise in the plane was full of joyful shouts and laughter. There was relief upon departure. Most of those on the plane had served their time in the service of their country and were definitely going home. For the others, they were on a 30 day leave before their next duty assignment.

For me that was the end of my active-duty obligation. I still had four more years of serving in the reserves, but that was not a full-time commitment. I had the desire to go on to school and take advantage of the GI Bill. Others wanted to return to their jobs and their life. Others wanted to go back to their families and reacquaint themselves. Most of us knew we were not the same and could never fully go back without acknowledging our past of combat, tenseness, and comradeship. All of us slept with our M16 for the year. Now even that was gone. Our language needed to be "cleaned-up" to adjust into civilian life. We had to be cleared to leave the Army and return back to our home of record. I was looking forward to it.

The lessons learned in the Army were significant. We learned how to lead and how to follow. We gained our confidence. There was no room for failure. There was a drive within us to do better things and to strive forward and be "Braves." We all earned our grey feathers and look forward to many other colors of noteworthy events in our lives. No longer would we be active military soldiers but instead civilians . Ahh, what a great feeling to be a civilian again!

The flight's first stopover was in Tokyo. The men were let off the plane to refresh themselves, purchase snacks and reading materials, and rest. The men were reassembled and embarked back to Seattle, Washington, or March Air Force base in California. Other air bases were used as well. Each man had to be cleared medically before beginning the journey to their hometown. Most received discharges from active service. Others who wanted to continue in the military received orders for their next assignment and received a leave to recuperate from the war.

On the next journey home on commercial aircraft, we had to wear our uniforms, but that was a minor thing. We went to the terminal awaiting our next flight. It did not matter how long the wait would be, we were ready for it.

The airplane arrived and boarding the plane was certainly different. It was full of civilians. There were a few military members on it, but most were not. The trip to our home seemed to take forever, especially after all that occurred in a year. Civilians were civil to us but did not talk to us. I am not sure why, but we did not know there about the war protests and its effort. We were not a popular group. Soldiers from the Vietnam War were not welcomed home, just tolerated. There were no parades celebrating return, no parties, and no recognition. It is as if the War did not happen. Our endurance, bravery, and effort during the war was not recognized by most. Only our family members recognized some of our contributions.

The plane landed and it was HOME. We were all excited to see our loved ones and families again. Active military was completed. A few of us will serve in the Reserves for a period of time, but that thought is not on our minds now.

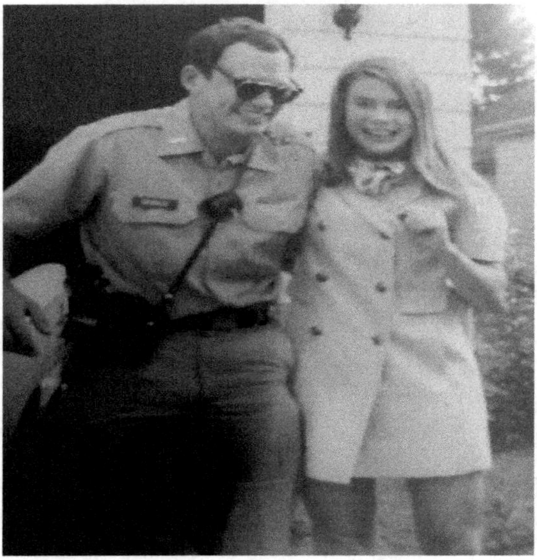

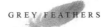

*Figure 30 Arriving Home after Deployment to Viet Nam*

In the next few weeks, I learned of the protests against the war. It seemed everything I remembered had changed. Even the terms people use had different meanings. Getting acclimated to the change was more difficult. I chose to go back to school for another degree program, rather than seek employment. The GI Bill covered Tuition and Room and Board, so it made it easier to go to school. I was not ready to work, as I was extremely nervous, and affected by loud sounds. Also, when sleeping , I would dream about the war, and shout out orders or plot how to defeat the enemy. This was an ongoing thing. As time went on, this too died down. Schooling provided me a way to settle down and prepare for what is next. A returning soldier is ready to learn, and I was that way also. School work was easier for me, and I could concentrate better. I was motivated to do well. The protests and the war were in the background now. I belonged as a civilian and could begin my career.

# Chapter Eight—Religions in Vietnam

Religions are an important facet of life in Vietnam. The types of the religions in Vietnam are the following:

- Christianity
- Animism
- Taoism
- Confucianism
- Buddhism
- Hoa Hao
- Cao Dai

All of these religions are a blend of beliefs in both form and practice. The differences may even vary from village to village, and province to province. Underlying all of these beliefs is a prevailing idea of ancestor veneration. Catholics may practice ancestor veneration. Buddhists may adhere to Confucianism principles and practices. However, Christianity beliefs and Buddhism practices may be unlike those in Thailand, and other countries.

The Viet Cong, guerilla warriors opposed to the current government, were well aware of the importance of religion in the everyday life of the Vietnamese. These "liberators" use the religious beliefs and practices in any way to help their cause; even though, most of the religious beliefs are not followed by the Viet Cong.

The United States Forces and their Allies also incorporated religious beliefs in their S-5 (Civic Action) activities to win the hearts and minds of the people in Vietnam. It is a part of the psychological warfare tool. It becomes a part of the operation when the enemy is sought out and to give the citizens of Vietnam an outlet to help the stamp out the rebellion and the terror resulting from it.

## CHRISTIANITY

Christianity dates back to the 16th century in Vietnam. The Roman Catholic Church sent a priest to South Vietnam. He went from village to village to talk to the people. His word spread, and today there are 11% of the population of Vietnam who call them Christians.

Roman Catholics are the largest group of Christians. Many missions were established in all areas of the country. Even the Vietnamese alphabet was developed by a priest by the name of Alexandre de Rhodes, S.J. who was in Vietnam from 1624 to 1654. It was and is a very influential religion in the country even today.

The Vietnamese culture practices the Roman Catholic faith in regard to their culture and surroundings. It is different from other countries, and as a practice has ancestral veneration incorporated in their religious beliefs. Today, the Roman Catholic Church is about ten per cent of the population and growing.

## PROTESTANTISM

The Protestant religion was established in Da Nang in 1911 by a Canadian missionary, Dr. R.A. Jaffray. He established a missionary which has over 100 missionaries in operation today. It is still continuing to operate today.

## ANIMISM

Animism is an outreach of the Montagnard religious belief. It is commonly referred to as the "people's religion." But what is animism? It is a belief in spirits that are both of dead persons and of inanimate objects. The spirit exists in persons even after death. Graves are provided with its needs and desires in its spirit state. If the graves are unattended, the spirits may become angry, bitter, or revengeful and may seek to re-enter the earthly life which they believe will call havoc in numerous ways.

The Animists associate the spirits with people. They believe them to be greedy, deceptive, unpredictable, and possessing of every trait known to man. Persons who die normally and have the proper rites said for them are believed to be sent happily on their way to the spirit world. Those that have untimely deaths (murder, suicide, accidents, war, tiger killings, woman who die in childbirth or die childless, and those bodies not recovered after death) anger the spirit world which becomes hostile to the family, to the individual, and to the community.

The Animist spends much of the time in observances and rites which will cause the spirits to do the will of the worshipper, and which will eliminate the spirits that can do him harm. Elaborate rituals and ceremonies are conducted. Offerings, sometimes including blood sacrifices, are made, accompanied by incantations and prayers. With events causing anxiety among the members, the village sorcerer is sought out for help to eliminate or remove the evil spirit that is affecting the event. Sickness and death are spirit-related, and members protect their children by giving them "unfavorable" nicknames, keeping the real names in confidence to decoy spirits away from the child.

Boys are more highly regarded than girls. If a boy is sickly, he may be dressed as a girl, or one earring put in a boy's ear to fold the spirits into thinking that the child is a girl. This is noticeable in the villages on the dress of the children.

# TAOISM

Taoism comes from China. The Dao is a road or way of life through which man attains harmony with nature as well as with the spiritual world. The worshippers accept all things as they are and adapts to the situations at hand. Most Tao worship, rituals, and ceremonies assist man to attune himself to the universe. All religious activities have a deep spiritual meaning. Also, Taoists believe that God's spirit can animate inanimate objects. The basic doctrines of Taoism are as follows:

- The universe including the nature of the physical and spiritual world is supreme.
- For every positive factor in the universe, there is an opposing negative force.
- The universe is controlled by a mystical supreme being from whom occasional mandates come to rulers or priests.
- The elements—metal, wood, water, fire, and earth—form the basis for the religious rites of Taoism.
- All factors exert influence on all facets of the Taoist's life.

Many of the basic beliefs of Taoism are incorporated into other religions. There is a limited formal organization of it in the country.

# Confucianism

This religion also came from China. It is part of the mixture of religions, with the three from China—Buddhism, Taoism, and Confucianism. Confucianism is part of the cultural environment in which they are born. They believe that the Confucius believed in continuing ancient rites and customs, with ethics being the chief contribution. Man is the measure of all things. Politics, ethics, education, and disciplines are combined with the spirit of reverence and devotion. Followers of Confucius stress the importance of good government and having harmonious relationships among all men. Man on the hand need to be more conscious of their obligations than of their rights.

The five obligations the followers of Confucius are charged are the following:

- Love and humanity
- Right actions expressing love and humanity
- Observation of the rites and/or rules of ceremony and courtesy
- Duty to be educated
- Self-confidence and fidelity toward others

Another Confucius principle is to have the children serve their parents. The principles of Confucianism continue in the daily lives of the people in Vietnam in education systems and family values.

# BUDDHISM

*Figure 31 Buddhist Temple*

Buddha teachings start by "Leading others, not by violence, but by righteousness and equity."

There are four noble truths in Buddhism. These are:

- The existence of life is a succession of suffering or to exist is to suffer.
- Suffering is caused by and created by desires or cravings.
- The elimination of suffering can be achieved only through the elimination of desire.
- The elimination of desire or craving can be achieved through the Noble Eightfold Path.

The Eightfold Path Principles are a way for the followers of Buddha to strive for perfection. The Eightfold Path Principles are as follows:

- Right views
- Right aspirations
- Right speech
- Right behavior
- Right living
- Right effort
- Right thoughts
- Right concentration
- Buddhism also has five Commandments or Provisions for their members to follow. These are:
- Do not kill
- Do not steal
- Do not be unchaste
- Do not lie
- Do not drink alcohol

Buddhism also has the Wheel of Karma. It is one of the earliest symbols and stands for the unending cycle of existence through which life goes on by birth and rebirth. The sum total of both good and bad actions that arise from thoughts, words, and deeds is the specific destiny in the next rebirth in the unending cycle of life. It is believed that all persons have Karma and that they are heirs of Karma.

Hinduism also believes in reincarnation, the wheel of existence, and Karma. Buddha believes there is no self and as a result no migration of the soul or community of the individual.

Buddhist followers want to aspire to achieve the state of Nirvana. Nirvana is the state of being freed from the cycle of rebirth or the Wheel of Existence. It is the final release from Karma and can be achieved only by long and laborious effort, self-denial, honorable deeds, thoughts, and purification through successive lives. Buddha is believed to have reached Nirvana as a result of the Enlightenment he received. There are many temples and pagodas built for the worship of Buddha.

## Hoa Hao

It is another form of Buddhism. It focuses on simplification of doctrine and practice. It is a part of the Thervada branch of Buddhism. The members have a background of military and political involvement. There is a lessened demand of its followers as the idea is to reduce the need for temples and pagodas, statues, monks, and other forms of Buddhism. Individual worship is the element for members to practice their religion.

Four major precepts of Hoa Hao are:

- Honor parents
- Love Country
- Respect Buddhism and its teachings
- Love fellow men

## Cao Dai

Buddhists do not recognize Cao Dai. The belief is that there is a tower-shaped throne of the Supreme Emperor. The major doctrines of Cao Dai are:

- It is the Third Revelation of divinity to all men and supersedes or corrects previous teachings.
- It worships the Absolute Supreme God who is eternal without beginning or end, who is the Creator of all and unique Master who created and creates all angels, Buddha's, and saints.
- It believes in the existence of invisible beings.
- The human soul may go up and down the ladder of existence.
- The ultimate goal is to deliver man from the endless cycle of existence.
- The worship of ancestry is a means of communication.
- Ethical concepts teach equality and brotherhood of all races.
- It recognizes a pantheon of saints and deities.
- It believes the divinity speaks to man through spiritual mediums

Vietnam is a truly diverse country and has variations in the practice of religion. While it is a rite and custom, the Viet Cong as a rule do not believe in these principles and beliefs.

# CHAPTER NINE–SUMMARY

The Vietnam War started under President John F. Kennedy in 1962 and ended with President Ford in 1975. Prior to 1962 President Eisenhower saw the need to send advisors into South Vietnam after the French were defeated at Dien Bien Phu in 1954.

This writing reflects the years of 1967, 1968, a1969 that the 3rd Battalion, 12th Infantry, 4th Infantry Division participated in the war effort. The unit was outstanding and had numerous award citations for its heroic efforts and determination to defeat the enemy.

It was a war that had two sides—political and military. The military side was well defined. It had strategies and tactics that worked. It had put together equipment, supplies, airplanes, naval ships, naval exploratory vessels, tanks, mechanized troop carriers, trucks, bulk carriers, cargo carriers, and supply chains, training of soldiers, successful coordination with ARVN troops and Allies, and profound military movements. The combat operations laid a foundation for years to come. We learned more about guerilla fighting, the role of Special Forces, and the role of combat through the use of helicopters and the coordinated effort with the Air Force and Navy.

The political side had many facets. A corrupt government of South Vietnam was heavily supported by money and support. It was detested by many in the country. The Communists were also detested, as they also stripped the villages of their men, their resources, and the viability. Politically, free fire zones were established which prevented US and Allies to return fire against the enemy. Holidays (free fire days) were imposed to give recognition to religious days, even though the enemy did not respect those days. There was a strong movement called civic action that wanted to "win the hearts and minds of the people." Yet, from the politicians, new warplanes were built, ships refurbished, Army and Marine equipment brought up to date, and a well-furnished supply chain was developed. A GI Bill program was put in place to help the returning soldier get more education and better skills to assimilate back into the job market. Veteran's hospitals received the wounded.

However political discussions to end the war after much success on the battlefields were not successful. Troop surges for combat were highly effective. But when it was all over and the war was ended thirteen years later (1962-1975) with the last troops withdrawing in 1975, South Vietnam fell to the North Vietnamese. Vietnam was no longer split between the South and the North. It was one country now under the control of the Hanoi government, supported by the Chinese. The US left dejected and demoralized on their loss. The military reorganized and again developed unprecedented strengths. Also, as an aftermath of the Vietnam War, the draft was never reinstated as a method of resupplying the military with troops. The services were now entirely voluntarily staffed. The reserves took on a new role. That role was to supplement the active services with reserve units when needed. The National Guard was also a part of the reserve movements when called.

# Bibliography

"The Ivy Leaf," Vol.4, Number 14, Newspaper, May 3, 1970

"The Ivy Leaf," Vol. 4, Number 3, Newspaper, February 1, 1970

"Espirit," Volume 1, Number 3, Magazine, Spring 1970

"Espirit," Volume 1, Number 2, Magazine Winter 1969

"Religions of Vietnam," Office of information, Command Information Pamphlet 1-70, January 1970.

"Led by Love of Country," Historical supplement, Daniel DeWald, January 1970, based on consolidated after action reports

"Gulf of Tonkin Resolution is Repealed Without Furor". *The New York Times.* January 14, 1971.

"Freedom of Information Past and Present". *NOW on PBS.* KQED. March 17, 2006. Retrieved May 16, 2012.

"Excerpts from Senate Debate on Tonkin Gulf Resolution". Vassar College. Wikisource: H.J. RES 1145

Moise, Edwin E. (1996). *Tonkin Gulf and the Escalation of the Vietnam War.* The University of North Carolina Press. ISBN 0-8078-2300-7.

"Combat Operations After Action Report," 3rd Battalion, 12th Infantry, 4th Infantry Division, 1969.

"Annual Historical Supplement," 3rd Battalion, 12th Infantry, 4th Infantry Division, 1967

"Combat After Action Report,' 3rd Battalion, 12th Infantry, 4th Infantry Division

# Drawing Schematics

# PICTURES

CPSIA information can be obtained
at www.ICGtesting.com
Printed in the USA
LVHW080819020622
720207LV00010B/298

9 781958 030141